MYSTERY QUILTS

Rita Fishel

American Quilter's Society
P. O. Box 3290 • Paducah, KY 42002-3290
www.AmericanQuilter.com

Located in Paducah, Kentucky, the American Quilter's Society (AQS) is dedicated to promoting the accomplishments of today's quilters. Through its publications and events, AQS strives to honor today's quiltmakers and their work and to inspire future creativity and innovation in quiltmaking.

EDITOR: TONI TOOMEY
GRAPHIC DESIGN: ELAINE WILSON
COVER DESIGN: MICHAEL BUCKINGHAM
QUILT PHOTOGRAPHY: CHARLES R. LYNCH
ALL OTHER PHOTOGRAPHY: ANDREW GIGLEY

Library of Congress Cataloging-in-Publication Data
Fishel, Rita.
Mystery quilts / by Rita Fishel.
p. cm.
Summary: "Quilts adapted to mystery-quilt events for groups such as teachers, guilds, retreats, cruises, recreation centers, and senior centers. Quilt tops can be completed in one or two afternoons and are simple enough for beginners with easy-to-follow instructions"--Provided by publisher.
ISBN 978-1-57432-917-9
1. Quilting--Patterns. I. Title.

TT835.F5665 2007
746.46'041--dc22
2006103315

Additional copies of this book may be ordered from the American Quilter's Society, PO Box 3290, Paducah, KY 42002-3290; 800-626-5420 (orders only please); or online at www.AmericanQuilter.com. For all other inquiries, call 270-898-7903.

COVER FROM LEFT TO RIGHT FIRST ROW: Elizabeth Tropf, Anita Harris; SECOND ROW: Diana Brewer, Judy Moyer; THIRD ROW: Shirley Schindler, Ruth Ann Wiley; BACK ROW: Mary Miller, Amie Litke, Kathy Wukela, Susie Stiving, Jill Smith, Kay Wallace

Dedication

This book is lovingly dedicated to my husband, Ron, and to my family. Without their constant encouragement and support this book never would have been possible.

To my best friend, Suzanne, who "tricked" me into writing a book and never let me rest. If she could beat leukemia, surely I could write a book!

To my customer and friend Tricia Eaton, who never closed an e-mail to me without encouraging me to "Keep writing."

And a special dedication and thanks goes to my dear friend, Julia Cleary. Without Julia my dream would not have been possible.

God bless you all.

Acknowledgments

Special thanks to the fabulous staff at Creations SewClever quilt shop in Chillicothe, Ohio:

Jan Bost
Vicki Rearly
Becky Wilson
Diane Adkins
Megan Poling
Carol Hixson

Linda Burton
Amy Rine
Stevie Jarvis
Susie Stiving
Becki Smith
Dawn Oyer

Rose Poling
Pam Herron
Carol Brady
Kay Appel
Peggy Carter

They are my closest friends, my best cheerleaders, and my quilting family. They constantly pick up the slack and allow me to venture beyond our walls. Going above and beyond their duties, they cut, stitched, pressed, and quilted all the wonderful quilts in this book. When they weren't working on the quilts, they were waiting on customers so others could be working on quilts. The quilts in this book were a united team by the Creations gang!

Master sleuths at Creations SewClever slumber party. **FROM LEFT TO RIGHT:** FIRST ROW: Linda Burton, Jan Bost, with baby Brenna, Carol Hixson; SECOND ROW: Susie Stiving, Carol Brady, Rita Fishel, Diane Adkins, Becky Wilson, Megan Poling-Detty, Vicki Rearly; BACK ROW: Becki Smith, Peggy Carter, Dawn Oyer, Stevie Jarvis, Kay Appel, Pam Herron, John Stiving

Contents

Introduction

Did you ever look at an old quilt and wish it could talk? What a story it could tell! I love to imagine the maker of the old quilt. Did she make it for someone special? Did it travel with a loved one who moved away? Think of the comfort that old quilt would have brought—memories of home and a tactile reminder of the love that its maker put into each and every stitch. Old quilts are like love letters that pass through generations, gathering more stories and more love as they're handed down.

Visit any quilt show and speak to the quilters. As they proudly show you their quilt, they tell you its story. Whether or not a quilt wins a ribbon is not the issue at the heart of a quilt show. When the quilter offers her quilt to the world to see, she is giving the world a glimpse into her soul.

Whenever I pick up a quilt I've made, it brings back memories of where I was when I was making it, whom I was with, what we were laughing about, and even perhaps the things that were going on in my life or within my family. Memories. Stitched from my heart, through my hands, and into every stitch of that quilt.

For years the Mystery Classes at my shop have encouraged new quilters, young and old. They come for the social event and for the food. They leave as quilters. It's a wonderful afternoon with food, friends, and fun. When each of the sleuths leaves a mystery class, they take their finished quilt top, a sense of satisfaction and accomplishment, and all the memories of that day spent making it.

This book is designed to make your quilting experience fun and simple. Each quilt pattern is intended to be completely cut and then sewn, without strip piecing, diagonal seams, or secondary cutting. The purpose of this approach is to make these patterns easy for the novice, and to make these patterns when quilting with a group of friends.

Each pattern is simply illustrated and can be made successfully with very little reading. My personal quiltmaking method has always been:

1. Look at the pictures.
2. Make the quilt top.
3. Rip it out.
4. Read the instructions.
5. Make the quilt top correctly.

My goal with this book is to eliminate the last three steps.

In reality, every quilt we make is a mystery until it is completed. We can only imagine our finished quilt. Even with the computerized designs and scanned fabric images, the colors, textures, and emotion in the quilt never come together completely until the last stitch is secured.

The patterns in the book have been designed to make lap-size mystery quilts. At the beginning of each mystery, I've given a hint to help you discover the name of the quilt. After you have followed the clues and pieced the top, you can go to the back of the book to find the solution to the mystery of the quilt's name. The solutions also give you the yardage requirements and instructions for adding the borders.

No day of quilting with friends is complete without some delicious food to help you keep up your energy. Throughout the book, I have included recipes for some of the favorite dishes served at my shop during our Mystery Classes. I hope you will soon get together with some quilting friends, pick a pattern from this book, and start sewing. Oh, and don't forget the food!

Tips for Successful Sleuthing

Before beginning, here are a few tips to assure success in your quilting adventure.

IDENTIFYING YOUR FABRICS

The fabrics in each mystery quilt are identified as feature, coordinate, contrast, background, and zingers. At the beginning of each pattern, a set of "mug shots" is given to help you match the fabric IDs to the clues for solving the mystery.

Feature fabric

This is the focus fabric in your quilt. All of the other fabric should work from this central piece. When you choose this piece, be aware of the size of the print and how it will appear when it has been cut. Try to keep your feature fabric print proportionate to the sizes of the pieces you will be cutting. Some of the quilt patterns utilize large pieces of feature fabric up to 8½" x 8½" squares. These will work well with the large floral prints and bold geometrics. In some of the patterns the feature fabrics are cut with widths as small as 3½". Medium to small prints work best for these pieces.

Another very important consideration is to note whether your fabric is directional. In some cases, with planned cutting and sewing, a directional print can be very effective. In other cases it can disrupt the overall design. Make sure to check the introduction to the fabric requirements in each pattern for any recommendations about directional prints.

Coordinate fabric (or fabrics)

The coordinate fabric (or fabrics) blends closely with the feature fabric. The tone should be quite similar to that of the feature fabric. Neither the feature fabric nor the coordinates should grab your attention one more than another.

Contrast fabric

The contrast fabric should be noticeably stronger than the feature or the coordinates. This is the fabric that will give your finished quilt some character.

Background fabric

We generally think of the background fabric as being white or a light neutral that is lighter than all the others in a quilt. However, if your feature print has a significant amount of light background in it, consider choosing a background fabric that has color to it. As a rule, it is safest to choose a background fabric that is not too busy. You don't want this piece to compete with your feature fabric. A subtle tone-on-tone print will usually make your quilt more interesting; however, be sure the background only plays a supporting role to the feature fabric.

Zinger fabric

This is the piece of fabric chosen to make your design pop. It is usually brighter or darker than all the other fabrics in the quilt. Not every pieced top has a zinger, but frequently one can be used in the border to give some added spark to your quilt. The zinger has a very strong personality. A little bit goes a long way. Be sure that whatever your choice, the zinger works with and brings out the best in the other fabrics in your quilt.

Possible choices for the contrast fabric

Possible choices for the coordinate fabric

Feature fabric

Possible background fabric

Fig. 1. Begin with the feature fabric, then choose possibilities for the coordinate and the contrast fabrics.

CHOOSING YOUR FABRICS

If you are unsure about combining fabrics, study the various quilts pictured in this book. In most cases I started with the feature fabric and then selected the colors in the print that I wanted to emphasize in the rest of the quilt. Ask a friend to help you, or have your local quilt shop work with you. With the feature fabric as the focal point, try a wide variety of fabrics, and notice how the feeling of the fabric combination changes. The feature fabric in figure 1 is a bright multi-color floral. I've chosen three possible coordinate colors that pick up colors in the feature fabric. The candidates for the contrast fabric pick up two of the darker colors in the feature fabric. Finish by choosing a tone-on-tone white or light neutral for the background fabric.

Try to play with several possibilities when planning a new quilt. Figure 2 shows a few of the possible combinations from the fabrics in figure 1. I find that if I lay a variety of fabric choices on the floor and walk into another room, when I come back and look at the fabric combinations with a fresh eye I can immediately see which combinations don't work and which ones I like.

Fig. 2. Possible combinations of fabrics

Tip from a Super Sleuth
TRACKING YOUR SUSPECTS

Labeling your groups of fabrics as you cut them will help you identify the pieces when you begin to stitch your quilt top. This is especially useful if you do your cutting long before you have the time to piece the top.

Don't be afraid of color! This is the perfect opportunity to experiment and play. Be creative. Be joyful. Be bold. This is the time to try colors that have intrigued you. Remember, there is no wrong color combination if it pleases you.

What a difference ¼" makes

Keeping a consistent ¼" seam allowance throughout the quilt top will make all of the pieces fit together. Your regular presser foot is usually not a ¼" from the needle to the edge of the foot. Most machine manufacturers offer a special foot for sewing accurate ¼" seams (fig. 3). Consider getting one of these feet for your quilting.

If you do not have a ¼" presser foot, a piece of masking tape on your sewing machine bed will do the trick. Place an acrylic ruler under the presser foot, with the ¼" line directly beneath the needle (fig. 4). Place a strip of masking tape along the right edge of the acrylic ruler. Be sure you don't cover your feed dogs with this tape. Now, use the left edge of the tape as your ¼" guide for the seam allowances in your quilts.

Chain stitching

Chain stitching makes piecing a quilt go very quickly. Instead of backstitching at the beginning and end of each seam, shorten the stitch length on your machine to 2. This is short enough not to pull out easily when you are manipulating the blocks, yet large enough to be able to rip out if necessary.

After you sew the first seam, leave the presser foot down and feed in the next pair of fabrics to be sewn. You can continue adding pairs to the chain for as long as you like. When the last pair is sewn, clip the chain apart and press the seams as instructed (fig. 5).

Fig. 3. Examples of ¼" presser feet used by quilters

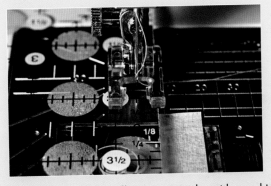

Fig. 4. Make a seam allowance guide with masking tape placed ¼" from the needle.

Fig. 5. Feed pieces continuously to create a chain.

Tip from a Super Sleuth
JOINING SEAMS

To reduce bulk and make the seams lie flat, be sure to rotate your strips so seams are going in opposite directions where they meet.

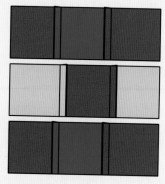

Arrange seams going in opposite directions.

Press as you go

Pressing makes all the difference in the final look of your quilt. I cannot express strongly enough how important it is to press your seam allowances as you complete each step. To get nice, flat seams, it is not necessary to stretch the fabrics as you press, but be sure to press well. Press the seam allowances in one direction. Work with steam on the wrong side of the fabric. Use your iron to hold the block in place as you gently and evenly tug the opposite end of the fabric (fig. 7). This prevents little pleats of excess fabric in the seams. Tugging too hard on the fabric will cause it to stretch and distort with the steam.

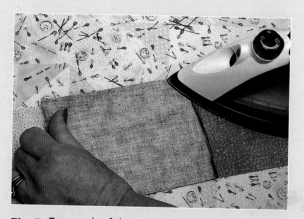

Fig. 7. Tug on the fabric very gently as you press the seam allowances together in one direction.

Tip from a Super Sleuth
PRESSING SEAMS IN THE RIGHT DIRECTION

As you complete each clue, pay close attention to the pressing instructions. If you always press the seam allowances in the recommended direction, your seams will lie flat when you join the blocks and rows.

Rita's Lazy Chicken Salad

This recipe puts a tangy twist on traditional chicken salad. It's so quick to make, I hardly notice I've been in the kitchen.

1 store-cooked rotisserie chicken, skinned, boned, and shredded with a fork
2 ribs celery, chopped
½ cup Craisins® (cranberry raisins)
½ cup Miracle Whip Light®
½ cup light sour cream
½ cup salsa of your choice
2 tbsp grape jelly

Mix all of the ingredients together and chill. May be served as sandwiches or on lettuce as salad. This makes enough for 8 hungry quilters.

Tips for Teaching Novice Sleuths

USING THE PATTERNS IN THIS BOOK

All the patterns in this book are designed to be successful for entry-level quilters. Cutting is straightforward, illustrations are visual, pieces are fairly large, and there's no diagonal piecing.

If you will be working with the novice and are considering a complete class in quilt piecing, the patterns in this book lend themselves perfectly! Beginning with the section on choosing fabrics, it will be easy to guide the inexperienced student through the process by following the very simplified steps in making color choices.

If you choose to have your students begin with the sewing, and bypass the cutting entirely (often done with children, seniors, or those with limited dexterity), you might consider having them use precut kits. You can allow them to choose fabrics themselves, then have the kits ready for the next class session, or you can strictly teach this as a machine-piecing class. These patterns work particularly well for sewing-only groups as there is no strip-piecing or secondary cutting required.

Instruct your students in the hows and whys of machine piecing as they work through the pattern chosen for the class. They can be taught to chain piece for added speed, and should be instructed in the proper method of pressing so as not to distort the blocks, nor pleat extra fabric in the seams.

When you're instructing beginners about adding borders to their pieced tops, I don't advise that you encourage them to sew the border, then trim the excess. Novice quilters tend to stretch the top piece of fabric as they sew long strips of fabric together, resulting in a quilt that is not straight or square. Rather, teach them how to measure the long sides, cut the border strips, quarter the sides and the strips, then ends, center, and quarter-marks. Teach them to sew the two long borders on the quilt and press the seams toward the newly added border. Then have them measure again, this time across the top and bottom of the quilt, to include the added border and continue as before. In a perfect world, the side measurements are equal to each other, as are the top and bottom. With beginning quilters this is rarely the case. Usually you can find a happy medium and make those measurements come out equal. Remember, in the end, it's not about perfection, it's about enjoying the process!

ABOVE: *How is this?* Amanda Howell

LEFT: *I need just the right backing.* Sharon Shuler, Susan Day

BELOW: *Is this the way?* Susan Day

WHAT IS A WENCH, AND HOW CAN I GET ONE?

Quilting with a group of friends is fun. If you're lucky enough to be the one hosting the quilt gathering, whether for a Mystery Class, a quilt retreat, a guild event, or a gang of gals hanging out for an afternoon or a weekend of quilt bonding, it's to your benefit, as well as the benefit of the group, if you do everything you can to assure that the event will be fun and productive.

In our shop, when we host a Mystery Class, we encourage extreme beginners to attend the event. Most often these beginners come with a friend or relative. Frequently these newbies are nervous and a bit intimidated, imagining they'll never be successful with something as challenging as sewing a quilt top. If left to their own devices, their worst fears would soon be realized. Often the one who has drafted this newbie feels responsible and thus spends her sewing time assisting the novice. I ask you, "Where's the fun in that?"

Wenches to the rescue! You can call this person (or persons, depending on your needs) anything you want. In our shop a wench is the quilt assistant who does all the ripping and pressing for those making the quilts. Wench requirements are: patience, a sense of humor, knowledge of the pattern being made (or the ability to interpret that pattern), skill with a seam ripper, and ability with an iron. It would probably be a good idea if this wench can sew, but the most important quality by far is that she be a willing spirit. A willing wench can make worlds of difference in the success of your quilting event!

The one thing you want to avoid, more than anything in your quilt affair, is any negativity. Quilters, especially novices, tend to get very discouraged when they make mistakes involving the R-word (ripping!). It's seen as personal failure. We simply can't allow that!

Wenches rip happily because there's no emotional attachment to the work. A good wench will soothe the sad quilter and assure her that she didn't fail! A great wench will respond immediately to the distressed quilter before the she knows she's sad.

Wenches are everywhere! We use customers who've done many Mystery quilts with us. They do the wenching so they can join in the fun and the food, without the cost of the class. They work for a free Mystery kit. Often when I work with guilds, wenches are guild members who would rather not drag their machine to a workshop, but want to enjoy the camaraderie of quilting friends. Sometimes the committee hosting the quilting event does all of the wenching for those attending. Whatever it takes, make it an honor to be a wench! The good ones are worth their weight in quilt fabric!

TOP ABOVE: *Wench brigade.*
Rita Fishel, Becki Smith

ABOVE: *Too busy to eat!*
Kay Wallace, LaRae Sorrell

Wench to the rescue!
Janet Drake, Kay Wallace

The Mysteries

Name tags help identify sleuths. Jan Bost

MYSTERY CLASS ANECDOTES
My Favorite One!

One of our enthusiastic sleuths was a new quilter who came to our town as a traveling nurse assigned to our local hospital. Since many of the nurses at the hospital are quilters, our visitor soon became hooked on quilting. Betty took any class she could fit into her schedule. This worked out to be a lot of classes, since she was lonely and had all her evenings free. We suggested she take a Mystery Class, because she'd complete a quilt top, meet some fun quilters, and get a wonderful meal! She signed up immediately.

Mystery Class began. All the sleuths were busy following clues and completing their quilt tops. Betty sewed with a vengeance!

As each top was completed and the mystery solved, the pressing wenches held up the quilts to the combined "oooooh's" and "ahhhh's" of the quilters. Finally, Betty finished her top. One of the willing wenches took her top to the ironing board while Betty chatted with all her neighbors at the sewing table. Eventually, the wench held up Betty's quilt with a flourish and said, "Look at this beautiful top. Isn't this grand?"

Betty looked up from her conversation and cried loudly, "Ohhhhh! My goodness! That is simply my favorite quilt!! Who made that one?"

I looked up from cutting borders, backings, and bindings and commented dryly, "Good thing you like it, Betty, because it's yours!"

Mr. Goodwench

A customer of ours, Jason, had recently begun taking quilting classes at the shop. He signed up to be a buddy for his sister, who wanted to learn to quilt. Although she never caught the bug, Jason was hooked from his first class! He completed several quilts, and I figured, since he had talent and to give him a financial break, I'd ask him to "wench" for us at one of the Mystery classes. He had no idea what a wench was. I explained that his job would be to press, rip, and encourage the sleuths.

"Well, I guess I could do that," he said reluctantly.

I introduced him to his table of six quilters as Mr. Goodwench. Hours later, Jason came up to the cutting table where I was busy cutting borders, backings, and bindings. I looked up at him questioningly.

"Hey," he said.

"Uhmmm," I replied as I cut more borders.

"What's with these women?" he asked.

"What do you mean?" I queried.

"Well, I have a $150 machine and just learned to quilt. The machines the ladies at my table are using are all over $2,000.00. That makes me think they probably know how to quilt."

"So, what's the problem?" I asked.

"All I have done is rip and explain all over again what they need to do!"

"Jason, Jason, Jason … you simply don't understand," I replied as I put the rotary cutter down. "You need to realize, these women did not come here to make a quilt. They came to hang out for an afternoon with girlfriends and good food; to laugh and sew and forget their obligations for a day. It's your job to see that they go home with a quilt top."

"Oh," he said. "I didn't know that."

? New Solution

I was teaching a Mystery Class at a rural Methodist church. The day was lots of fun. The women all knew each other well and provided a wonderful carry-in lunch. Most of them were comfortable with a sewing machine, and everything was moving along smoothly. Thank goodness, as I was the only wench! After lunch these sleuths really got into their work. They chatted and laughed, and one or two kept me pretty busy with the seam ripper, but all seemed to be going well.

As the day wore down, quilt tops were being completed, and the excitement was rising, as energy was beginning to wane. Everyone, it seemed, could see the possibility of truly finishing a quilt top in one afternoon. I was allowing myself to relax a bit and appreciate how well this large class had gone, despite not having extra wenches to assist, when I heard my name being paged plaintively from the other side of the room. "Uh-oh," I thought to myself as I went to see what the problem was. "Apparently I counted my luck too soon." Spread across the floor were the blocks that had been completed by our distressed quilter, and all had been assembled incorrectly. I could see that ripping and re-stitching were not going to be

BELOW LEFT: *Is this right?* Janet Drake

BELOW RIGHT: *I'll race you!* Sharon Shuler, Susan Day

acceptable. I quickly and cheerily said, "Oh, don't be upset! Remember, these are mystery quilts. Let's see what these detectives can discover." A couple of us arranged her blocks several ways until we found a new pattern. "Wow!" she exclaimed delightedly. "Who'd have guessed there were two solutions to this mystery!"

Bring Your Own Machine

Generally when we teach classes at our shop, we suggest the student bring his or her own machine. It's just easier to take a class on a machine you're familiar with, rather than try to learn a machine and a new technique at the same time. However, if a student doesn't have a machine, has a very old machine in poor running order, or has a cabinet-model machine, we have machines that they can borrow.

Melissa enthusiastically signed up for a Mystery Class by herself. She had never attended, had no friends who quilted, and thought this would be a fun way to learn. We agreed, because besides being fun, it's instant gratification since you take home a finished quilt top. She asked if she needed to bring her own machine, and without any question we said that would be best.

To my complete surprise, the morning of the Mystery a big truck pulled up to the back door of the shop. I knew we weren't expecting a delivery— it was Sunday!

I went to the door to see what was happening and out jumped Melissa from the passenger side. Her patient husband got out of the cab and came around to the back of the truck where he unloaded a great big, heavy, ancient sewing machine. I was pretty near speechless. "Well, at least it's electric," I thought. Melissa and hubby just smiled and said, "Morning," as he helped her carry her machine in to the classroom.

Where's the Beef?

I often take my Mystery show on the road, because it provides a fun day of sewing for the quilters in attendance. They can visit, laugh, and relax, yet still complete the project before the day is over. When we have Mystery Classes at our shop, we provide a grand, four-course meal, and I swear some of the sleuths come just to meet 'n eat. The fact that they leave with a finished quilt top is icing on their cake.

I had a Mystery Class scheduled with a guild about *two and a half* hours from our shop. I thought we had everything worked out. I took precut kits, a mini-shop for them to browse, irons, ironing boards, extension cords, and extra machines. I filled the Stitch Mobile. Imagine my surprise when, after I spent about an hour unloading the van and setting up the classroom, several of the sleuths said, "So where's the food?"

Perhaps the next Stitch Mobile should be a catering truck!

It Might Be a Heart Attack

Wilma works nights and comes to the Mystery Classes with little or no sleep. This may contribute to her less-than-stellar sewing. She runs a sewing machine like our neighbor drives his plow—fast and over anything in the way.

One Mystery Sunday, Wilma was even more discombobulated than normal. She'd spent the night at the hospital as they tried to determine if she'd had a heart attack.

"So, did they tell you you're okay?" I asked with some trepidation.

"Oh, they couldn't tell me anything. I have to go back for more tests," she said.

"Then, you don't know whether the pains you had were heart-related?" I inquired.

"Nope. And believe me, that's making me real nervous," she grumbled.

The class was moving along, having fun solving mysteries, but I never took my eyes off Wilma. Due to the extra stress, her piecing was worse than normal. When the wench took Wilma's completed top to press, she called me aside and said in a horrified voice, "Rita, look! Most of her seams are full of holes."

"Wilma!" I called. "Look at your beautiful quilt top!" I held it up and swung it around for everyone to admire—and so no one would notice all the holes where seams should be. "Now, don't you think you should go home and get some rest?"

The next day I sent Wilma's quilt top home with an employee to be repaired. Later, when Wilma came to get her quilted and bound Mystery quilt, she showed it off with pride to the shop staff. "Isn't this just fabulous?" she quipped. "I thought I was having a heart attack that day, and I still managed to make a perfect quilt top!"

Four in One Afternoon!

Frequently, I'm asked to teach a Mystery class off-site. I happily take my show on the road if it makes it easier for the sleuths. I usually cut quite a few more kits than we have sleuths, so they have a nice assortment from which to choose. Often, after completing one top in the class, sleuths will buy one or two more kits to take home with them, since they're completely precut and make up quickly.

I had a huge room full of about thirty sleuths, all seated in one large circle facing the center of the room. It's rare that we ever have enough room to set up a group that size, but it was fun because they could all chatter and compete with each other. As the day went on, one quilter in particular sewed like she was driven by demons. She hardly looked up to chatter, and I'm not sure if she ever took a break for lunch. By the time we had a little less than an hour left to sew, she came up for air. I said, "I'm simply amazed with how focused (obsessed?) you are with your project!"

She replied, "I have six kids. I get nothing done at home. This is my time to do something for me. I'm having a ball!"

As it neared 5:00 p.m. and we began to put things away, she jumped up and shouted, "Four! I got four Mystery tops done!" Her friends gave her a standing ovation. I guess she wins.

Virtual Quilting

Our shop secretary, fondly called Nut-Meg (not to confuse her with my daughter, My-Meg) began working for us while she was still in high school. She was a computer tech and came to work as part of a class assignment, and God Bless her, she never left! She's been with us almost seven years now.

During all those years, she has truly become part of our gang. She never showed the least interest in quilting, but she picked up the lingo and answered questions over the phone as if she were a pro. I joke that she learned to quilt by osmosis.

As I began to publish patterns for my Mystery quilts, I lacked the computer skills to make the patterns look professional. Give me a paper and pencil (with a big eraser) any day, but please don't make me do anything but e-mail on a computer! I watched with amusement as Meg would "rotary cut" the pattern pieces in the computer quilt program. She struggled to line up seams and trim off excess "fabric." It fascinated me, since she was learning my skill with sewing tools on a computer screen!

Recently, Meg announced she was going to have a baby. We were as excited as twenty grammas could be! We decided that, for her baby gift, we would cut a beautiful baby quilt pattern and then have her sit down and sew it. She was nervous! She was intimidated! She was thrilled! She was a natural! She caught on quickly, and after proudly making her little Brenna's baby quilt, she developed quilting fever. She is on her third quilt in four months! Computers come and computers go ... but quilting lives forever!

Legend of the Spinning Top

This cheerful little quilt is a snap to make! As you stitch it together remember childhood summers, filled with endless, carefree sunny days and simple delights like playing cards clipped to bicycle spokes, bubble pipes, inflatable wading pools, and bright twirling toys blown by the wind.

THE SUSPECTS

Should you choose to use directional fabrics in this pattern, as long as you pay attention to placement as you sew, your pattern will come out fine. It's not recommended that you use a directional fabric for your background.

All of the first cuts should be done with the fabric folded, selvage-to-selvage, as it comes off the bolt. Be sure to remove all selvage edges before making the first cuts.

Fingerprinting the Suspects

To fingerprint your suspects, arm yourself with a pen and a pad of sticky notes. Keep your suspects in groups as you cut them, and label the groups according to their fabric ID and piece sizes, as given in the List of Suspects.

SOLVING THE MYSTERY

Line up your groups of fingerprinted suspects. Set your machine for a stitch length of 2, and be sure you are able to sew consistent ¼" seams. Remember, it is all right if the seam allowances are not exactly ¼", as long as they are consistent. Plug in your iron, and don your sleuth cap!

Use the mug shots and the clues that follow to solve the mystery and identify the culprit. You will find the solutions to the mysteries on pages 62–91.

feature   light background   dark contrast

MUG SHOTS

Pieced top, 48" x 60"

LIST OF SUSPECTS			
Fabric ID	**Yardage**	**First Cut**	**Second Cut**
Feature	¾ yd.	4 strips 6½" x 40"	20 squares 6½" x 6½"
Light Background	1½ yd.	8 strips 6½" x 40"	80 rectangles 3½" x 6½"
Dark Contrast	1 yd.	8 strips 3½" x 40"	80 squares 3½" x 3½"
Yardage based on 40" fabric width			
Additional fabric requirements for the borders, batting, backing, and binding are given in the solutions on pages 62–91.			

Legend of the Spinning Top

Clue 1. Make 80.

❋Clue 1 **1.** Gather eighty 3½" x 3½" contrast squares and eighty 3½" x 6½" background rectangles. Press the seam allowances toward the background rectangle. Make 80.

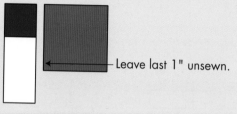

—Leave last 1" unsewn.

Clue 2. Make 20.

❋Clue 2 **1.** Gather the twenty 6½" x 6½" feature squares and twenty strips completed in clue 1. **2.** Look carefully at clue 2. Place one of the strips completed in step one along one side of a feature square. The edge of the contrast square should be even with the edge of the feature square as shown. **3.** Sew these together stopping 1" before the bottom edge of the feature square. Press the seam allowances toward the feature square.

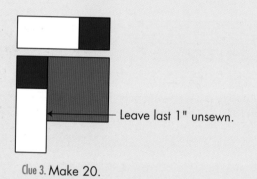

—Leave last 1" unsewn.

Clue 3. Make 20.

❋Clue 3 **1.** Gather 20 more strips completed in clue 1 and the 20 units completed in clue 2. **2.** Working clockwise around the feature square, sew the new strip to the next edge of the feature square. Be sure to sew the strip so the contrast square is not touching the contrast square of the strip already on the feature block. Press seam allowances toward the strips. Make 20.

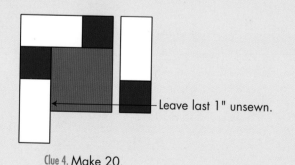

—Leave last 1" unsewn.

Clue 4. Make 20.

❋Clue 4 **1.** Gather 20 more strips completed in clue 1. **2.** Sew the new strip to the next available side of the feature square as shown. Pay close attention to the position of the contrast square. Press the seam allowance toward the strips. Make 20.

✳Clue 5 **1.** Gather the remaining 20 strips completed in clue 1 and the units from clue 4. **2.** Sew the new strip to the last side of the feature square, again paying close attention to the position of the contrast square. Press the seam allowances toward the strips. **3.** Finish sewing the 1" opening left in clue 1 to the feature block, and continue the seam along the edge of the contrast bar from the last strip. Press all seams away from the feature square.

Clue 5. Make 20.

✳Clue 6 **1.** Gather the 20 completed units from clue 5. **2.** Assemble five rows as shown. Press the seam allowances in one direction.

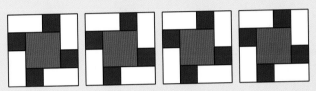

Clue 6. Make 5.

✳Clue 7 **1.** Lay out the rows completed in clue 6. Rotate every other row so the seam allowances are going in opposite directions. **2.** Examine the solutions on pages 62–91 to find the quilt photo and assembly diagram that match your suspect. Sew the rows together and press well. Add the borders and complete your quilt as described in your quilt's solution page.

🔍 **Tip from a Super Sleuth**

When cutting multiple layers of fabric, stack the fabrics, place your ruler to cut, reach across the ruler with your rotary cutter, and cut the last inch of your strip. This will anchor your fabrics so they won't scoot. Now cut through all the layers, as usual.

Chain-piece for speed! Connie Grounds, Connie Leimbach

Quick Crab Dip

1¼ c. mayonnaise
1 c. crabmeat
½ c. grated Cheddar
1 tbsp. horseradish
¼ c. French dressing

Mix all together. Chill. Serve with crackers.

Mystery in the Antique Sewing Chest

This pattern with an old-fashioned name makes a particularly great baby or child's quilt! It works up quickly and easily and is great with bright, cheery prints. Lightning bolts lead in both directions like a favorite trim that never grows old. Bright or dark fabrics placed beside the feature fabric grab your interest and lead your eye.

THE SUSPECTS

Your suspects will be cut from fabrics identified in the cutting list. For suggestions on fabric selection, see Identifying Your Fabrics on pages 7–8. To keep this quilt simple, avoid obvious directional prints. For your zinger, choose a fabric with a bold personality that will bring out the best in the other fabrics and make the pattern pop.

All of the first cuts should be done with the fabric folded, selvage-to-selvage, as it comes off the bolt. Be sure to remove all selvage edges before making the first cuts.

Tracking your suspects

Arm yourself with a pen and a pad of sticky notes. Keep your suspects in groups as you cut them, and label the groups according to their fabric ID and piece sizes, as given in the List of Suspects.

SOLVING THE MYSTERY

Line up your groups of suspects. Set your machine for 10–15 stitches per inch (usually a setting of 2). Plug in your iron and don your sleuth cap!

Use the mug shots of your suspects to help you follow the clues to solving the mystery. Be sure to sew with a consistent ¼" seam allowance. You will find the solutions to the mystery quilts on pages 62–91.

feature   coordinate A   coordinate B   zinger

MUG SHOTS

Pieced top, 48" x 60"

LIST OF SUSPECTS			
Fabric ID	**Yardage**	**First Cut**	**Second Cut**
Feature	1 yd.	7 strips 4½" x 40"	20 rectangles 12½" x 4½"
Coordinate A	⅔ yd.	5 strips 4½" x 40"	20 rectangles 4½" x 8½"
Coordinate B	⅔ yd.	5 strips 4½" x 40"	20 rectangles 4½" x 8½"
Zinger	⅔ yd.	5 strips 4½" x 40"	40 squares 4½" x 4½"
Yardage based on 40" fabric width			
Additional fabric requirements for the borders, batting, backing, and binding are given in the solutions on pages 62–91.			

✴Clue 1 **1.** Gather 20 coordinate-A rectangles and 20 zinger squares. **2.** Sew one zinger square to one end of each coordinate-A rectangle. Press the seam allowances toward the zingers. Make 20.

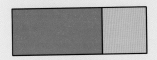

Clue 1. Make 20.

✴Clue 2 **1.** Gather the 20 units completed in clue 1. **2.** Sew two strips completed in clue 1 together lengthwise as shown. Pay close attention to the positions of the zingers. Make sure the zinger squares are on opposite ends, with the top zinger on the left. Press the seam allowances in either direction. Make 10.

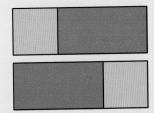

Clue 2. Make 10.

✴Clue 3 **1.** Gather the 10 units completed in clue 2 and 10 feature rectangles. **2.** Sew one feature rectangle to each unit as shown. Press the seam allowances toward the feature rectangles. This is block A. Make 10.

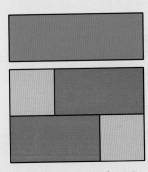

Clue 3. Block A: Make 10.

✴Clue 4 **1.** Gather 20 coordinate-B rectangles and the remaining 20 zinger squares. **2.** Sew one zinger square to one end of each coordinate-B rectangle. Press the seam allowances toward the zingers. Make 20.

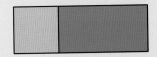

Clue 4. Make 20.

✴Clue 5 **1.** Gather the 20 units completed in clue 4. **2.** Sew two strips completed in clue 4 together lengthwise as shown. Pay close attention to the positions of the zingers. Make sure the zinger squares are on opposite ends, with the top zinger on the right. Press the seam allowances in either direction. Make 10.

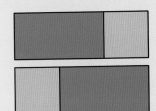

Clue 5. Make 10.

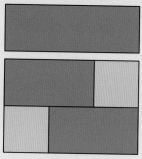

Clue 6. Block B: Make 10.

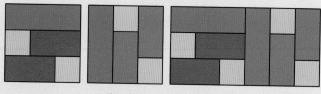

Clue 7. Row X: Make 3.

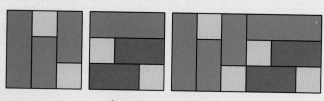

Clue 8. Row Y: Make 2.

✳Clue 6 **1.** Gather the 10 units completed in clue 5 and the remaining 10 feature rectangles. **2.** Sew one feature rectangle to each unit as shown. Press the seams allowances toward the feature rectangles. This is block B. Make 10.

✳Clue 7 **1.** Gather six A blocks and six B blocks. **2.** Assemble three rows, as shown, alternating the blocks beginning with an A block and ending with a B block. Pay close attention to the positions of the blocks. Make sure the A blocks are set horizontally and the B blocks are set vertically. Press the seam allowances toward the B block at the end of each row. This is row X.

✳Clue 8 **1.** Gather four A blocks and four B blocks. **2.** Assemble two rows, as shown, alternating the blocks beginning with a B block and ending with an A block. Pay close attention to the positions of the blocks. Make sure the B blocks are set vertically and the A blocks are set horizontally. Press the seam allowances toward the first B block in each row. This is row Y.

✳Clue 9 **1.** Lay out the complete X and Y rows, alternating the rows beginning and ending with an X row. Sew the rows together and press well. **2.** Examine the solutions on pages 62–91 to find the quilt photo and assembly diagram that match your completed quilt top. Add the borders and finish your quilt as described in your quilt's solution page.

🔍 Tip from a Super Sleuth

To most efficiently press all those mystery seams (wenches, pay attention!), press from the wrong side of the quilt pieces; use steam; use the iron as a counter-weight, and tug gently (not to distort!) on the fabrics to be sure you aren't pressing "pleats" into the seams. Double-check your work by pressing a second time from the right-side of the quilt pieces.

Clues Along the Uneven Path

This is a wonderful pattern to begin your travels in quilting. Pieces are relatively big and layout is quite simple. It's a particularly good pattern for large-scale prints. Follow the meandering roads and enjoy a delightful journey.

THE SUSPECTS

Your suspects will be cut from fabrics identified in the cutting list. For suggestions on fabric selection, see Identifying Your Fabrics on pages 7–8. If you choose directional fabrics, pay close attention to the picture of this completed quilt. As you assemble the blocks, make sure the directional prints are facing the same way. Of course, this means you will need to solve the mystery and find the quilt in the solutions on pages 62–91 before you begin making your quilt top.

All of the first cuts should be done with the fabric folded, selvage-to-selvage, as it comes off the bolt. Be sure to remove all selvage edges before making the first cuts.

Tracking your suspects

Arm yourself with a pen and a pad of sticky notes. Keep your suspects in groups as you cut them, and label the groups according to their fabric ID and piece sizes, as given in the List of Suspects.

SOLVING THE MYSTERY

Line up your groups of suspects. Set your machine for 10–15 stitches per inch (usually a setting of 2). Plug in your iron and don your sleuth cap!

Use the mug shots of your suspects to help you follow the clues to solving the mystery. Be sure to sew with a consistent ¼" seam allowance. You will find the solutions to the mystery quilts on pages 62–91.

feature   dark contrast   light background   medium coordinate

MUG SHOTS

Pieced top, 48" x 60"

LIST OF SUSPECTS			
Fabric ID	**Yardage**	**First Cut**	**Second Cut**
Feature	1¼ yd.	5 strips 8½" x 40"	20 squares 8½" x 8½"
Dark contrast	½ yd.	3 strips 4½" x 40"	20 squares 4½" x 4½"
Light background	¾ yd.	3 strips 8½" x 40"	20 rectangles 4½" x 8½"
Medium coordinate	¾ yd.	3 strips 8½" x 40"	20 rectangles 4½" x 8½"
Yardage based on 40" fabric width			
Additional fabric requirements for the borders, batting, backing, and binding are given in the solutions on pages 62–91.			

Clues Along the Uneven Path

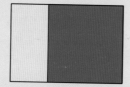

Clue 1. Make 20.

Clue 2. Make 20.

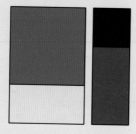

Clue 3. Make 20.

Clue 4. Row X: Assemble 3.

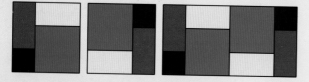

Clue 5. Row Y: Assemble 2.

Tip from a Super Sleuth

Any good wench knows she must be able to rip quickly! A hint for fast seam ripping is this: find the bobbin thread of the seam to be ripped, (it's usually the flatter-looking stitching) and snip that thread. Then you can often, carefully pull that thread to "unsew" the seam.

✳Clue 1 **1.** Gather the 20 feature squares and 20 light-background rectangles. **2.** Sew one light-background rectangle to each feature square. Press the seam allowances toward the feature squares.

✳Clue 2 **1.** Gather the 20 dark-contrast squares and medium-coordinate rectangles. **2.** Sew one dark-contrast square to the short side of each medium-coordinate rectangle. Press the seam allowances toward the rectangles.

✳Clue 3 **1.** Gather the 20 units completed in clue 1 and the 20 units completed in clue 2. **2.** Assemble 20 blocks as shown. Be sure each finished block matches the figure. Press the seam allowances in the same direction.

✳Clue 4 **1.** Gather 12 of the blocks completed in clue 3. **2.** Assemble three rows as shown. Press the seam allowances in the same direction. This is row X.

✳Clue 5 **1.** Gather the remaining eight blocks completed in clue 3. **2.** Assemble two rows as shown. Press the seam allowances in the same direction. This is row Y.

✳Clue 6 **1.** Lay out rows X and Y, alternating the rows, beginning and ending with an X row. Sew the rows together and press well. **2.** Examine the solutions on pages 62–91 to find the quilt photo and assembly diagram that match your completed quilt top. Add the borders and finish your quilt as described in your quilt's solution page.

Secret in the Bureau Drawer

This quilt will warm your heart and your toes. The quilt makes up quickly and is a great pattern for the man in your life. Make it from flannel and it will be even cozier.

THE SUSPECTS

Your suspects will be cut from fabrics identified in the cutting list. For suggestions on fabric selection, see Identifying Your Fabrics on pages 7–8. Directional prints are not recommended for this pattern.

All of the first cuts should be done with the fabric folded, selvage-to-selvage, as it comes off the bolt. Be sure to remove all selvage edges before making the first cuts.

Tracking your suspects

To fingerprint your suspects, arm yourself with a pen and a pad of sticky notes. Keep your suspects in groups as you cut them, and label the groups according to their fabric ID and piece sizes as given in the List of Suspects.

SOLVING THE MYSTERY

Line up your groups of suspects. Set your machine for 10–15 stitches per inch (usually a setting of 2). Plug in your iron and don your sleuth cap!

Use the mug shots of your suspects to help you follow the clues to solving the mystery. Be sure to sew with a consistent ¼" seam allowance. You will find the solutions to the mystery quilts on pages 62–91.

feature   background   contrast

MUG SHOTS

Pieced top, 45" x 63"

LIST OF SUSPECTS			
Fabric ID	**Yardage**	**First Cut**	**Second Cut**
Feature	1½ yd.	2 strips 9½" x 40"	8 squares 9½" x 9½"
		4 strips 3½" x 40"	36 squares 3½" x 3½"
Background	1½ yd.	3 strips 9½" x 40"	9 squares 9½" x 9½"
		4 strips 3½" x 40"	36 squares 3½" x 3½"
Contrast	½ yd.	9 strips 3½" x 40"	90 squares 3½" x 3½"
Yardage based on 40" fabric width			
Additional fabric requirements for the borders, batting, backing, and binding are given in the solutions on pages 62–91.			

Secret in the Bureau Drawer

Clue 1. Make 18.

Clue 2. Make 36.

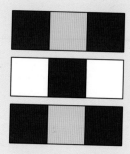

Clue 3. Make 18.

Clue 4. Row X: Make 4.

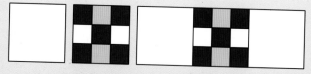

Clue 5. Row Y: Make 3.

✳Clue 1 **1.** Gather thirty-six 3½" x 3½" background squares and 18 contrast squares **2.** Sew two background squares to opposite sides of each contrast square. Press the seam allowances in one direction. Make 18.

✳Clue 2 **1.** Gather thirty-six 3½" x 3½" feature squares and the remaining 72 contrast squares. **2.** Sew two contrast squares to opposite sides of each feature square. Press the seam allowances in one direction. Make 36.

✳Clue 3 **1.** Use the strips completed in clues 1 and 2 to make 18 Nine-Patch blocks, as shown. Press the seam allowances in one direction.

✳Clue 4 **1.** Gather eight 9½" x 9½" feature squares and 12 Nine-Patch blocks completed in clue 3. **2.** Assemble four rows as shown. Alternate the blocks, beginning and ending with a Nine-Patch block. Be sure the 3½" feature squares meet the large feature squares at each seam. Press the seam allowances toward the large feature squares. This is row X.

✳Clue 5 **1.** Gather nine 9½" x 9½" background squares and the remaining six Nine-Patch blocks. **2.** Assemble three rows as shown. Begin and end each row with a background square. Be sure the 3½" background squares meet the large background squares at each seam. Press the seam allowances toward the large background squares. This is row Y.

🔍 Tip from a Super Sleuth

When cutting kits for all of your sleuths, it speeds up the sewing process, (and makes for happy detectives!) if you remove all selvages from the border strips! We also suggest that you use sticky labels to identify each fabric and shape for the kits.

✱Clue 6 **1.** Lay out the X and Y rows, alternating the rows, beginning and ending with an X row. Sew the rows together and press well. **2.** Examine the solutions on pages 62–91 to find the quilt photo and assembly diagram that match your completed quilt top. Add the borders and finish your quilt as described in your quilt's solution page.

Clue three, clue three, clue three... Sharon Shuler

Light and Tasty Summer Rice & Veggie Salad

This is delicious as an accompaniment for sandwiches or as a main-dish salad with lots of finger foods. I use frozen veggies whenever possible to cut down on preparation time.

2 cups uncooked rice
   (*I like to mix brown, white, and wild*)
10 oz. bag frozen, chopped broccoli
   (*rinse in warm water to thaw, then drain*)
1½ cups frozen chopped onions and peppers
   (*rinse in warm water and drain*)
1 cucumber, partially peeled and diced
1–2 fresh tomatoes, seeded and chopped
¾ cup orange juice
¼ cup lemon juice
½ cup olive oil
½ cup crumbled feta cheese

In 3 cups of water and a dash of salt, cook rice (uncovered) on high until vent holes appear. Turn to lowest setting (or off on electric stove) and cover tightly. Allow to steam for about 10 more minutes or until fluffy. While the rice cools, prepare the rest of the ingredients. Toss everything together and top with crumbled feta cheese. Serves 6 sleuths.

Solved! **FROM LEFT TO RIGHT:** Susan Day, Pam Wysong, Margaret Bradshaw

Strength for the journey! **FROM LEFT TO RIGHT:** Pam Patrick, Vicki Rearley, Kay Wallace, LaRae Sorrell

What Was in the Demin Jacket?

This simple quilt mimics the weave in a popular fabric that perhaps everyone has worn at one time or another. It's as casual and as comfortable as your favorite pair of jeans. Pull on this quilt when you want to curl up in your favorite chair, with a good book, a cup of hot chocolate, and a long sigh.

THE SUSPECTS

Your suspects will be cut from fabrics identified in the cutting list. For suggestions on fabric selection, see Identifying Your Fabrics on pages 7–8. For the light background, it's best to use a non-directional fabric and one that will not dramatically reveal its seam lines. If you choose a directional fabric, pay close attention to the way the background squares are sewn to the feature rectangles. As you assemble the rows, make sure the directional prints are going the same way.

All of the first cuts should be done with the fabric folded, selvage-to-selvage, as it comes off the bolt. Be sure to remove all selvage edges before making the first cuts.

Tracking your suspects

Arm yourself with a pen and a pad of sticky notes. Keep your suspects in groups as you cut them, and label the groups according to their fabric ID and piece sizes, as given in the List of Suspects.

SOLVING THE MYSTERY

Line up your groups of suspects. Set your machine for 10–15 stitches per inch (usually a setting of 2). Plug in your iron and don your sleuth cap!

Use the mug shots of your suspects to help you follow the clues to solving the mystery. Be sure to sew with a consistent ¼" seam allowance. You will find the solutions to the mystery quilts on pages 62–91.

feature   background   contrast

MUG SHOTS

Pieced top, 48" x 66"

LIST OF SUSPECTS			
Fabric ID	**Yardage**	**First Cut**	**Second Cut**
Feature	1¼ yd.	3 strips 12½" x 40"	18 rectangles 6½" x 12½"
		1 strip 3½" x 40"	6 rectangles 3½" x 6½"
Light background	1⅓ yd.	3 strips 6½" x 40"	17 squares 6½" x 6½"
		4 strips 6½" x 40"	40 rectangles 3½" x 6½"
Dark contrast	½ yd.	5 strips 3½" x 40"	48 squares 3½" x 3½"
Yardage based on 40" fabric width			
Additional fabric requirements for the borders, batting, backing, and binding are given in the solutions on pages 62–91.			

✳Clue 1 **1.** Gather 12 large feature rectangles and eight light-background squares. **2.** Assemble four rows, beginning and ending with a large feature rectangle as shown. Press the seam allowances toward the light squares. This is row A.

Clue 1. Row A: Assemble 4.

✳Clue 2 **1.** Gather the nine light squares, six large feature rectangles, and six small feature rectangles. **2.** Assemble three rows beginning and ending with a small feature rectangle as shown. Press the seam allowances toward the light squares. This is row B.

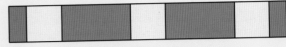

Clue 2. Row B: Assemble 3.

✳Clue 3 **1.** Gather all 48 contrast squares and 40 light-background rectangles. **2.** Assemble eight rows with five light rectangles and six contrast squares beginning and ending with a contrast square as shown. Press the seam allowances toward the contrast squares. This is row C.

Clue 3. Row C: Assemble 8.

✳Clue 4 **1.** Gather three A rows, three B rows, and six C rows. **2.** Sew four rows in the following order as shown: C row, A row, C row, B row. Press the seam allowances toward the right in the first two groups and toward the left in the third group. Assemble three groups.

Clue 4. Assemble 3.

✳Clue 5 **1.** Gather the remaining A row and the two remaining C rows. Sew them as shown. Press the seam allowances toward the left.

Clue 5. Assemble 1.

✳Clue 6 **1.** Lay out the groups from clues 4 and 5, arranging the them so the seam allowances are going in opposite directions. Sew the groups together and press well. **2.** Examine the solutions on pages 62–91 to find the quilt photo and assembly diagram that match your completed quilt top. Add the borders and finish your quilt as described in your quilt's solution page.

🔍 Tip from a Super Sleuth

If you make any of these Mystery patterns and want a quick finish for a lap quilt, cut borders as follows: 1st border – 6 strips cut 1½" wide; 2nd border – 7 strips cut 4½" wide; binding – 7 strips cut 3" wide. Voila!

Message in the Needlework

Needlework has never been faster or easier than with this charming quilt pattern. In the time it takes you to thread a needle, you can have this delightful quilt pieced and ready for quilting. Give your eyes and fingers a rest and enjoy this "needlework."

THE SUSPECTS

Your suspects will be cut from fabrics identified in the cutting list. For suggestions on fabric selection, see Identifying Your Fabrics on pages 7–8. If you choose directional fabrics, pay close attention to the picture of this completed quilt, so the directional fabrics are facing the same way as the blocks and rows are sewn together. Of course, this means you will need to solve the mystery and find the quilt in the solutions on pages 62–91 before you begin making your quilt top.

All of the first cuts should be done with the fabric folded, selvage-to-selvage, as it comes off the bolt. Be sure to remove all selvage edges before making the first cuts.

Tracking your suspects

Arm yourself with a pen and a pad of sticky notes. Keep your suspects in groups as you cut them, and label the groups according to their fabric ID and piece sizes, as given in the List of Suspects.

SOLVING THE MYSTERY

Line up your groups of suspects. Set your machine for 10–15 stitches per inch (usually a setting of 2). Plug in your iron and don your sleuth cap!

Use the mug shots of your suspects to help you follow the clues to solving the mystery. Be sure to sew with a consistent ¼" seam allowance. You will find the solutions to the mystery quilts on pages 62–91.

feature   coordinate   contrast

MUG SHOTS

Pieced top, 48" x 60"

LIST OF SUSPECTS			
Fabric ID	**Yardage**	**First Cut**	**Second Cut**
Feature	1¼ yd.	4 strips 6½" x 40"	20 squares 6½" x 6½"
		4 strips 3½" x 40"	40 squares 3½" x 3½"
Coordinate	1¼ yd.	4 strips 6½" x 40"	20 squares 6½" x 6½"
		4 strips 3½" x 40"	40 squares 3½" x 3½"
Contrast	1 yd.	8 strips 3½" x 40"	80 squares 3½" x 3½"
Yardage based on 40" fabric width			
Additional fabric requirements for the borders, batting, backing, and binding are given in the solutions on pages 62–91.			

✻Clue 1 **1.** Gather the forty 3½" x 3½" feature squares and forty 3½" x 3½" contrast squares. **2.** Sew the feature and contrast squares in pairs as shown. Press the seam allowances toward the contrast square. Make 40. **3.** Gather the remaining forty 3½" x 3½" contrast squares and forty 3½" x 3½" coordinate squares. **4.** Sew the contrast and coordinate squares in pairs as shown. Press the seam allowances toward the contrast square. Make 40.

Clue 1, step 2. Make 40.

Clue 1, step 4. Make 40.

✻Clue 2 **1.** Gather all of the pairs completed in clue 1. **2.** Sew one of each pair into a Four-Patch unit as shown. Make sure the contrast squares are opposite each other on the diagonal. Press the seam allowances in the same direction. Make 40.

Clue 2. Four-Patch: Make 40.

✻Clue 3 **1.** Gather 20 Four-Patch units completed in clue 2 and the twenty 6½" x 6½" feature squares. **2.** Sew these together as shown. Pay close attention to this step, making sure to position the small feature square in the Four-Patch unit next to the upper-left corner of the large feature square. Press the seam allowances toward the feature squares. This is unit A.

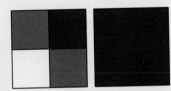

Clue 3. Unit A: Make 20

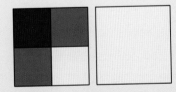

Clue 4. Unit B: Make 20.

✻Clue 4 **1.** Gather the remaining 20 Four-Patch units, and the twenty 6½" x 6½" coordinate squares. **2.** Sew these together as shown. Pay close attention to this step, making sure to position the small coordinate square in the Four-Patch unit next to the lower-left corner of the large coordinate square. Press the seam allowances toward the feature squares. This is unit B.

Do those seams match? Amanda Howell

Message in the Needlework

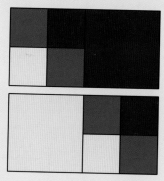

Clue 5. Make 20.

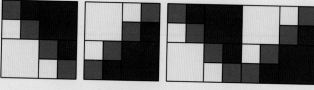

Clue 6. Row X: Make 3.

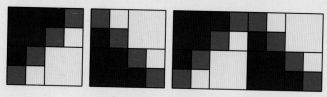

Clue 7. Row Y: Make 2.

✱Clue 5 **1.** Gather all of the A and B units completed in clues 3 and 4. **2.** Join one of each unit as shown. Pay close attention to the positions of the large feature and coordinate squares. Press the seam allowances in any direction.

✱Clue 6 **1.** Gather 12 blocks completed in clue 5. **2.** Assemble three rows of blocks as shown. Pay close attention to the position of each large feature square in each row. Also make sure the contrast blocks step up in the correct direction. Press the seam allowances toward the feature squares. This is row X.

✱Clue 7 **1.** Gather the remaining eight blocks completed in clue 5. **2.** Assemble two rows of blocks as shown. Pay close attention to the position of each large feature square in the row. Also make sure the contrast blocks step down in the correct direction. Press the seam allowances toward the feature squares. This is row Y.

✱Clue 8 **1.** Lay out the X and Y rows, alternating the rows, beginning and ending with an X row. Sew the rows together and press well. **2.** Examine the solutions on pages 62–91 to find the quilt photo and assembly diagram that match your completed quilt top. Add the borders and finish your quilt as described in your quilt's solution page.

Tip from a Super Sleuth

If you'd like to add a "zinger" to your lap quilt, without adding inches to your finished top, cut six 1" strips of a "zinger" fabric. Seam them together to form one long strip. Press seams open. Press in half lengthwise, right-side-out. Stitch this, raw-edges-together, around the edge of your first border, then add the outer border to your quilt.

Strawberry Slaw

3 cups bagged slaw
2 cups cantaloupe and/or strawberries
1 tbsp. honey in ⅓ cup poppyseed dressing

Toss gently together and chill before serving.

The Deserted Highway

This charming quilt is a variation on the CROSS STITCH quilt pictured on page 72. It was designed especially for a guild that requested its own unique Mystery. I had only 24 hours to design a quilt, and already had pieces cut for CROSS STITCH. I hope you enjoy this road as much as my guild friends!

THE SUSPECTS

Your suspects will be cut from fabrics identified in the cutting list. For suggestions on fabric selection, see Identifying Your Fabrics on pages 7–8. If you choose directional fabrics, pay close attention to the picture of this completed quilt, so the directional prints are facing the same way as you sew the blocks and rows together. Of course, this means you will need to solve the mystery and find the quilt in the solutions on pages 62–91 before you begin making your quilt top.

All of the first cuts should be done with the fabric folded, selvage-to-selvage, as it comes off the bolt. Be sure to remove all selvage edges before making the first cuts.

Tracking your suspects

Arm yourself with a pen and a pad of sticky notes. Keep your suspects in groups as you cut them, and label the groups according to their fabric ID and piece sizes, as given in the List of Suspects.

SOLVING THE MYSTERY

Line up your groups of suspects. Set your machine for 10–15 stitches per inch (usually a setting of 2). Plug in your iron and don your sleuth cap!

Use the mug shots of your suspects to help you follow the clues to solving the mystery. Be sure to sew with a consistent ¼" seam allowance. You will find the solutions to the mystery quilts on pages 62–91.

feature   coordinate   contrast

MUG SHOTS

Pieced top, 48" x 60"

LIST OF SUSPECTS			
Fabric ID	**Yardage**	**First Cut**	**Second Cut**
Feature	1¼ yd.	4 strips 6½" x 40"	20 squares 6½" x 6½"
		4 strips 3½" x 40"	40 squares 3½" x 3½"
Coordinate	1¼ yd.	4 strips 6½" x 40"	20 squares 6½" x 6½"
		4 strips 3½" x 40"	40 squares 3½" x 3½"
Contrast	1 yd.	8 strips 3½" x 40"	80 squares 3½" x 3½"

Yardage based on 40" fabric width

Additional fabric requirements for the borders, batting, backing, and binding are given in the solutions on pages 62–91.

The Deserted Highway

Clue 1, step 2. Make 40.

Clue 1, step 4. Make 40.

Clue 2. Four-Patch unit: Make 40.

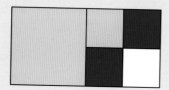

Clue 3. Unit A: Make 20.

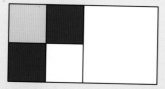

Clue 4. Unit B: Make 20.

✳Clue 1 **1.** Gather forty 3½" x 3½" feature squares and forty 3½" x 3½" contrast squares. **2.** Sew the feature and contrast squares in pairs as shown. Press the seams toward the contrast squares. **3.** Gather the remaining 40 contrast squares and forty 3½" x 3½" coordinate squares. **4.** Sew the contrast and coordinate squares in pairs, as shown. Press the seams toward the contrast squares.

✳Clue 2 **1.** Gather all of the pairs from clue 1. **2.** Sew one of each pair into a Four-Patch unit, as shown. Make sure the contrast squares are opposite each other on the diagonal. Make 40.

✳Clue 3 **1.** Gather 20 of the completed Four-Patch units and the twenty 6½" x 6½" feature squares. **2.** Sew these together as shown. Pay close attention to this step, making sure to position the small feature square in the Four-Patch unit against the upper-right corner of the large feature square. Press the seam allowances toward the feature squares. This is unit A.

✳Clue 4 **1.** Gather the remaining 20 Four-Patch units and the twenty 6½" x 6½" coordinate squares. **2.** Sew these together as shown. Again, pay close attention, making sure to position the small coordinate square in the Four-Patch unit against the lower-left corner of the large coordinate square. Press the seam allowances toward the feature squares. This is unit B.

🔍 Tip from a Super Sleuth

Next time you host a Mystery class for friends, guild members, or customers, have a "theme party." Ask sleuths to dress in theme costume and make the food and decorations theme-appropriate. Give prizes for best costume!

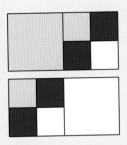

Clue 5. Make 20.

✱**Clue 5** **1.** Gather all of the A and B units completed in clues 3 and 4. **2.** Join one of each unit as shown. Pay close attention to the positions of the large feature and coordinate squares. Press the seam allowances in any direction.

✱**Clue 6** **1.** Gather 12 blocks from clue 5. **2.** Assemble three rows of blocks as shown. Pay close attention to the position of the large feature squares in the row. Also, make sure the contrast blocks step upward. Press the seam allowances toward the feature fabrics. This is row X.

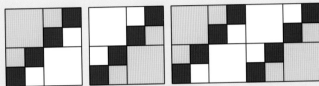

Clue 6. Row X: Make 3.

✱**Clue 7** **1.** Gather the remaining eight blocks completed in clue 5. **2.** Assemble two rows of blocks as shown. Pay close attention to the position of the large feature squares in the row. Also make sure the contrast blocks step upward. Press the seam allowances toward the feature fabrics. This is row Y.

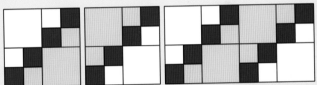

Clue 7. Row Y: Make 2.

✱**Clue 8** **1.** Lay out rows X and Y. Alternate the rows, beginning and ending with an X row. Sew the rows together and press well. **2.** Examine the solutions on pages 62–91 to find the quilt photo and assembly diagram that match your completed quilt top. Add the borders and finish your quilt as described in your quilt's solution page.

Beach blanket bingo babes! Mary Miller, Sherri Jenkins

Apple Broccoli

3 cups broccoli florettes
1 chopped Granny Smith apple
1 bag shredded carrots
⅓ cup golden raisins

Toss with Marzetti® Slaw Dressing and ½ tsp. dill weed.

The Baffling Basket Case

This intricate-looking pattern is easy as can be. Made from only two blocks, it goes together in a jiffy. Try making this from fabrics that have a textured appearance, such as marbles or rich tone-on-tone prints. It's simply beautiful and beautifully simple.

THE SUSPECTS

Your suspects will be cut from fabrics identified in the cutting list. For suggestions on fabric selection, see Identifying Your Fabrics on pages 7–8. Directional prints are not recommended for this pattern. All of the first cuts should be done with the fabric folded, selvage-to-selvage, as it comes off the bolt. Be sure to remove all selvage edges before making the first cuts.

Tracking your suspects

Arm yourself with a pen and a pad of sticky notes. Keep your suspects in groups as you cut them, and label the groups according to their fabric ID and piece sizes, as given in the List of Suspects.

SOLVING THE MYSTERY

Line up your groups of suspects. Set your machine for 10–15 stitches per inch (usually a setting of 2). Plug in your iron and don your sleuth cap!

Use the mug shots of your suspects to help you follow the clues to solving the mystery. Be sure to sew with a consistent ¼" seam allowance. You will find the solutions to the mystery quilts on pages 62–91.

| feature | coordinate | contrast |

MUG SHOTS

Pieced top, 54" x 63"

LIST OF SUSPECTS			
Fabric ID	**Yardage**	**First Cut**	**Second Cut**
Feature	1½ yd.	4 strips 9½" x 40"	42 rectangles 3½" x 9½"
		4 strips 3½" x 40"	42 squares 3½" x 3½"
Coordinate	1½ yd.	11 strips 3½" x 40"	42 rectangles 3½" x 9½"
		4 strips 3½" x 40"	42 squares 3½" x 3½"
Contrast	½ yd.	4 strips 3½" x 40"	42 squares 3½" x 3½"
Yardage based on 40" fabric width			
Additional fabric requirements for the borders, batting, backing, and binding are given in the solutions on pages 62–91.			

✳Clue 1 1. Gather 21 contrast squares and 42 coordinate squares. **2.** Sew two coordinate squares to opposite sides of each contrast square as shown. Press the seam allowances in one direction. Make 21.

Clue 1. Make 21.

✳Clue 2 1. Gather the 21 strips completed in clue 1 and 42 feature rectangles. **2.** Sew two feature rectangles to the top and bottom of each strip from clue 1. Press the seam allowances toward the feature rectangles. This is block A.

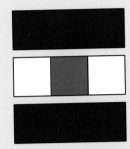

Clue 2. Block A: Make 21.

✳Clue 3 1. Gather 21 contrast squares and 42 feature squares. **2.** Sew two feature squares to opposite sides of each contrast square as shown Press the seam allowances in one direction. Make 21.

Clue 3. Make 21.

✳Clue 4 1. Gather the 21 strips completed in clue 3 and 42 coordinate rectangles. **2.** Sew two coordinate rectangles to the top and bottom of each strip from clue 3. Press the seam allowances toward the coordinate rectangles. This is block B.

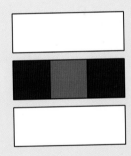

Clue 4. Block B: Make 21.

✳Clue 5 1. Gather 12 A blocks and 12 B blocks. **2.** Referring to figure 6, sew six blocks together, alternating blocks, beginning with an A block. Notice that the A blocks are always vertical, while the B blocks are always horizontal. **3.** Press the seam allowances toward the A blocks. Make four rows. This is row X.

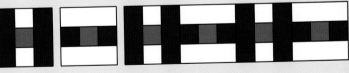

Clue 5. Row X: Make 4.

The Baffling Basket Case

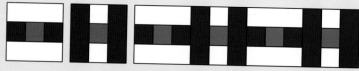

Clue 6. Row Y: Make 3.

✳Clue 6 1. Gather nine A blocks and nine B blocks. **2.** Referring to figure 7, sew six blocks together, alternating blocks, beginning with a B block. Notice that the A blocks are always vertical, while the B blocks are always horizontal. **3.** Press the seam allowances toward the A blocks. Make three rows. This is row Y.

✳Clue 7 1. Lay out the rows from clues 5 and 6, beginning and ending with a row X. Sew the rows together and press well. **2.** Examine the solutions on pages 62–91 to find the quilt photo and assembly diagram that match your completed quilt top. Add the borders and finish your quilt as described in your quilt's solution page.

Chicken Barley Salad

I like to serve dishes that are filling, yet mild, that appeal to most people's taste. This will go a long way and everyone loves it.

2 cups pearl barley

4½ cups water

dash salt

½ tsp olive oil

1 store-cooked rotisserie chicken, skinned, boned and shredded with fork (or 6 boneless, skinless chicken breasts, roasted and shredded with fork)

1 cup frozen corn

1 cup frozen peppers and onions

1 medium can black beans, rinsed and drained

1–2 fresh tomatoes, chopped

¼ cup olive oil

⅛ cup balsamic vinegar

¾ cup favorite salad dressing

1 cup shredded cheese or feta cheese

In a large sauce pan over high heat, bring barley, water, salt, and olive oil to a boil. Stir periodically. Allow to boil on high until most of the water is absorbed. Cover, turn to low, and continue to cook until all water is absorbed (like rice). While the barley is cooking, rinse the frozen corn, peppers, and onions in warm water to thaw, then drain. When the barley is done, let it cool, then add the remaining ingredients. Toss gently and chill before serving. Serves 6 sleuths.

Chat 'n sew. FROM LEFT TO RIGHT: Ruth Ann Wiley, Judy Moyer, Diana Brewer

Secret in the Sewing Box

This pattern lends itself well to the use of large, soft floral fabrics. Weave through them a prominent ribbon of fabric for a romantic look. Or, encourage a masculine appeal by selecting flannels or plaids. Whatever you choose, you can be certain this pattern will weave together simply and the finished quilt will warm the heart of the recipient.

THE SUSPECTS

Your suspects will be cut from fabrics identified in the cutting list. For suggestions on fabric selection, see Identifying Your Fabrics on pages 7–8. Directional prints are not recommended for the background and coordinate fabrics.

All of the first cuts should be done with the fabric folded, selvage-to-selvage, as it comes off the bolt. Be sure to remove all selvage edges before making the first cuts.

Tracking your suspects

Arm yourself with a pen and a pad of sticky notes. Keep your suspects in groups as you cut them, and label the groups according to their fabric ID and piece sizes, as given in the List of Suspects.

SOLVING THE MYSTERY

Line up your groups of suspects. Set your machine for 10–15 stitches per inch (usually a setting of 2). Plug in your iron and don your sleuth cap!

Use the mug shots of your suspects to help you follow the clues to solving the mystery. Be sure to sew with a consistent ¼" seam allowance. You will find the solutions to the mystery quilts on pages 62–91.

feature   background   coordinate A   coordinate B

MUG SHOTS

Pieced top, 50" x 56"

LIST OF SUSPECTS			
Fabric ID	**Yardage**	**First Cut**	**Second Cut**
Feature	1½ yd.	3 strips 2½" x 40"	34 squares 2½" x 2½"
		5 strips 8½" x 40"	34 rectangles 4½" x 8½"
Background	1 yd.	3 strips 8½" x 40"	18 rectangles 4½" x 8½"
		2 strips 4½" x 40"	17 rectangles 2½" x 4½"
Coordinate A	⅔ yd.	5 strips 4½" x 40"	36 squares 4½" x 4½"
Coordinate B	⅔ yd.	5 strips 4½" x 40"	36 squares 4½" x 4½"
Yardage based on 40" fabric width			
Additional fabric requirements for the borders, batting, backing, and binding are given in the solutions on pages 62–91.			

Secret in the Sewing Box

Clue 1. Make 17.

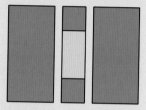

Clue 2. Block A: Make 17.

Clue 3. Make 36.

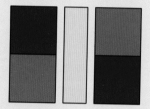

Clue 4. Block B: Make 18.

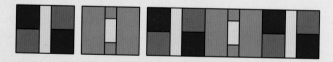

Clue 5. Row X: Make 4.

Tip from a Super Sleuth

If you are hosting a Mystery class for newbies, be sure they don't bring quilting thread to machine piece their mystery quilt!

✳Clue 1 **1.** Gather the 34 feature squares and seventeen 2½" x 4½" background rectangles. **2.** Sew one feature square to opposite ends of the background rectangles. Press the seam allowances in one direction. Make 17.

✳Clue 2 **1.** Gather the 34 feature rectangles and the 17 strips completed in clue 1. **2.** Sew a feature rectangle to each side of a strip as shown. Press the seam allowances toward the large feature rectangles. This is block A. Make 17.

✳Clue 3 **1.** Gather 36 coordinate-A squares and 36 coordinate-B squares. **2.** Sew these into pairs as shown. Press the seam allowances toward the darker squares. Make 36 pairs.

✳Clue 4 **1.** Gather the 36 coordinate pairs completed in clue 3 and 18 background rectangles. **2.** Sew one coordinate pair to each side of the background rectangle as shown. Pay close attention to the position of the coordinate A squares. They should be on upper left and lower right corners of the background rectangle. **3.** Press the seam allowances toward the background rectangles. This is block B. Make 18.

✳Clue 5 **1.** Gather eight A blocks and 12 B blocks. **2.** Sew four rows as shown. Alternate the blocks, beginning and ending with a B block. Press the seam allowances toward the feature rectangles. This is row X.

✳Clue 6 **1.** Gather nine A blocks and six B blocks. **2.** Assemble three rows as shown. Alternate the blocks, beginning and ending with an A block. This is row Y.

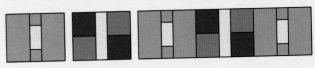

Clue 6. Row Y: Make 3.

✳Clue 7 **1.** Lay out the X and Y rows completed in clues 5 and 6. Alternate the rows, beginning and ending with an X row. Sew the rows together and press well. **2.** Examine the solutions on pages 62–91 to find the quilt photo and assembly diagram that match your completed quilt top. Add the borders and finish your quilt as described in your quilt's solution page.

Isn't it gorgeous? Mary MacCarter

Salsa Chicken and Rice

Chicken is usually a great staple when feeding crowds. It's economical and most people like it. The following recipe is delicious and could be part of an evening with a Mexican or Southwestern theme.

1½ cups long grain rice (I mix wild/brown/ long grain white.)

3 tbsp. olive oil

2 cups fresh mushrooms, sliced

1 onion, chopped

3 cups salsa (your choice)

1 medium can cream of chicken soup

8 oz. sour cream

1 medium can chicken broth

1 store-cooked rotisserie chicken, skinned, boned and shredded with fork (or 6 boneless, skinless chicken breasts, roasted and shredded with fork)

Sauté chicken, onion, and mushrooms in olive oil until chicken is done. (If you use rotisserie chicken there is no need to sauté this with the onion and mushrooms, just add it with the rice, etc.) Combine this with the rice, salsa, soup, sour cream, and broth. Pour into 9" x 13" greased baking dish. Cover and bake at 350° for 45 minutes. Uncover and bake 10 more minutes. This will serve about 6 sleuths.

Unexpected Playground Clue

Here's a fun, simple quilt that goes together so quickly that it will seem like child's play. Dramatic and contrasting colors make this quilt especially appealing. Large prints work well in the big blocks. Enjoy the game.

THE SUSPECTS

Your suspects will be cut from fabrics identified in the cutting list. For suggestions on fabric selection, see Identifying Your Fabrics on pages 7–8. Directional prints are not recommended.

All of the first cuts should be done with the fabric folded, selvage-to-selvage, as it comes off the bolt. Be sure to remove all selvage edges before making the first cuts.

Tracking your suspects

Arm yourself with a pen and a pad of sticky notes. Keep your suspects in groups as you cut them, and label the groups according to their fabric ID and piece sizes, as given in the List of Suspects.

SOLVING THE MYSTERY

Line up your groups of suspects. Set your machine for 10–15 stitches per inch (usually a setting of 2). Plug in your iron and don your sleuth cap!

Use the mug shots of your suspects to help you follow the clues to solving the mystery. Be sure to sew with a consistent ¼" seam allowance. You will find the solutions to the mystery quilts on pages 62–91.

feature   light background   dark contrast

MUG SHOTS

Pieced top, 50" x 60"

LIST OF SUSPECTS			
Fabric ID	**Yardage**	**First Cut**	**Second Cut**
Feature	1 yd.	5 strips 6½" x 40"	30 squares 6½" x 6½"
Light background	1 yd.	4 strips 2½" x 40"	60 squares 2½" x 2½"
		4 strips 6½" x 40"	60 rectangles 2½" x 6½"
Dark contrast	1 yd.	4 strips 2½" x 40"	60 squares 2½" x 2½"
		4 strips 6½" x 40"	60 rectangles 2½" x 6½"
Yardage based on 40" fabric width			
Additional fabric requirements for the borders, batting, backing, and binding are given in the solutions on pages 62–91.			

✳Clue 1 **1.** Gather 58 light background squares and 58 contrast squares. **2.** Sew the light-background and contrast squares in pairs as shown. Press the seams toward the contrast squares.

Clue 1. Make 58.

✳Clue 2 **1.** Gather 40 of the pairs completed in clue 1. **2.** Sew the pairs into Four-Patch units as shown. Make sure the contrast squares are diagonally opposite each other. Press the seam allowances in one direction. Make 20.

Clue 2. Four-Patch unit: Make 20.

✳Clue 3 **1.** Gather 49 contrast rectangles and 49 light rectangles. **2.** Sew pairs of rectangles together along their long edges (fig. 4). Press the seam allowances toward the dark rectangles.

Clue 3. Make 49.

✳Clue 4 **1.** Gather six contrast rectangles, 12 units completed in clue 3, and 15 feature squares. **2.** Assemble three rows as shown. Begin and end each row with a contrast rectangle. Pay close attention to positions of the contrast rectangles in the units from clue 3. Press the seams in one direction. This is row A.

Clue 4. Row A: Assemble 3.

✳Clue 5 **1.** Gather six background rectangles, 12 units completed in clue 3, and 15 feature squares. **2.** Assemble three rows as shown. Begin and end each row with a background rectangle. Pay close attention to positions of the background rectangles in the units from clue 3. Press the seams in one direction. This is row B.

Clue 5. Row B: Assemble 3.

🔍 Tip from a Super Sleuth

If you are hosting a Mystery Quilt Party, especially if it's for beginners, be sure to have some "back-up" sewing machines on hand. Newbies sometimes forget the cord or foot pedal, or they dig Grannie's machine out of the basement and bring it to class, not knowing it's frozen-up and can't possibly sew!

Unexpected Playground Clue

Clue 6. Row C: Assemble 3.

Clue 7. Row D: Make 2.

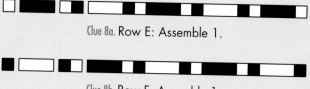

Clue 8a. Row E: Assemble 1.

Clue 8b. Row F: Assemble 1.

✳Clue 6 **1.** Gather 12 Four-Patch units completed in clue 2, 15 units completed in clue 3, and six units completed in clue 1. **2.** Assemble three rows as shown. Pay close attention to the positions of the contrast pieces. Press the seams in one direction. This is row C.

✳Clue 7 **1.** Gather eight Four-Patch units completed in clue 2, ten units completed in clue 3, and four units completed in clue 1. **2.** Assemble two rows as shown. Pay close attention to the positions of the contrast pieces. Press the seams in one direction. This is row D.

✳Clue 8 **1.** Gather the remaining contrast and background squares and rectangles, and the remaining units completed in clue 1. **2.** Assemble one of each row shown, paying close attention to the positions of the contrast pieces. Press the seams in one direction. These are rows E and F.

✳Clue 9 **1.** Lay out the rows in the following order: row E, row A, row C, row B, row D, row A, row C, row B, row D, row A, row C, row B, row F. Notice that every feature square is completely surrounded by either all background bars or all contrast bars. Sew the rows together and press well. **2.** Examine the solutions on pages 62–91 to find the quilt photo and assembly diagram that match your completed quilt top. Add the borders and finish your quilt as described in your quilt's solution page.

Quilting diva! Katrina Robinson

What Became of Aunt Emma's Pinafore?

This happy quilt is a unique way to showcase a large print fabric. Your zinger can be light or dark, because both will sparkle. Play around with color selection and be amazed at the different impact from the placement of dark and light fabrics.

THE SUSPECTS

Your suspects will be cut from fabrics identified in the cutting list. For suggestions on fabric selection, see Identifying Your Fabrics on pages 7–8. This pattern does not lend itself well to directional fabrics, unless the directional print is the feature fabric. For your zinger, choose a fabric with a bold personality that will bring out the best in the other fabrics and make the pattern pop.

All of the first cuts should be done with the fabric folded, selvage-to-selvage, as it comes off the bolt. Be sure to remove all selvage edges before making the first cuts.

Tracking your suspects

Arm yourself with a pen and a pad of sticky notes. Keep your suspects in groups as you cut them, and label the groups according to their fabric ID and piece sizes, as given in the List of Suspects.

SOLVING THE MYSTERY

Line up your groups of suspects. Set your machine for 10–15 stitches per inch (usually a setting of 2). Plug in your iron and don your sleuth cap!

Use the mug shots of your suspects to help you follow the clues to solving the mystery. Be sure to sew with a consistent ¼" seam allowance. You will find the solutions to the mystery quilts on pages 62–91.

feature   coordinate A   coordinate B   zinger
MUG SHOTS

Pieced top, 54" x 63"

LIST OF SUSPECTS			
Fabric ID	**Yardage**	**First Cut**	**Second Cut**
Feature	1½ yd.	3 strips 8½" x 40"	10 squares 8½" x 8½"
		2 strips 8½" x 40"	9 rectangles 4½" x 8½"
		1 strip 4½" x 40"	2 squares 4½" x 4½"
Coordinate A	1¼ yd.	4 strips 6½" x 40"	30 rectangles 4½" x 6½"
		2 strips 4½" x 40"	30 rectangles 2½" x 4½"
Coordinate B	1¼ yd.	4 strips 6½" x 40"	30 rectangles 4½" x 6½"
		2 strips 4½" x 40"	30 rectangles 2½" x 4½"
Zinger	⅜ yd.	2 strips 2½" x 40"	30 squares 2½" x 2½"

Yardage based on 40" fabric width

Additional fabric requirements for the borders, batting, backing, and binding are given in the solutions on pages 62–91.

What Became of Aunt Emma's Pinafore?

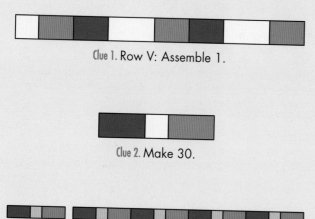

Clue 1. Row V: Assemble 1.

Clue 2. Make 30.

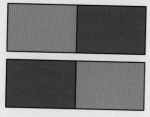

Clue 3. Row W: Assemble 6.

Clue 4. Make 25.

Clue 5. Make 6.

✳Clue 1

1. Gather one small feature square, two feature rectangles, three 4½" x 6½" coordinate-A rectangles, and two 4½" x 6½" coordinate-B rectangles. **2.** Assemble one row, beginning with the small feature square and ending with a coordinate-A rectangle as shown. Press the seam allowances toward the feature square. This is row V.

✳Clue 2

1. Gather thirty 2½" x 4½" coordinate-A rectangles, thirty 2½" x 4½" coordinate-B rectangles, and 30 zinger squares. **2.** Sew 30 units as shown. Press the seam allowances toward the coordinate-A rectangles. Make 30.

✳Clue 3

1. Gather all of the units completed in clue 2. **2.** Sew five units together end to end, beginning the row with a coordinate-B rectangle and ending with a coordinate-A rectangle as shown. Press the seams allowances in the same direction toward the coordinate-A rectangles. This is row W. Make six rows.

✳Clue 4

1. Gather twenty-five 4½" x 6½" coordinate-A rectangles and twenty-five 4½" x 6½" coordinate-B rectangles. **2.** Sew 25 pairs of rectangles together lengthwise as shown. Press the seam allowances toward the coordinate-A rectangles.

✳Clue 5

1. Gather 12 of the units completed in clue 4. **2.** Sew six units as shown. Make sure the coordinate-A rectangles are positioned as shown. Press the seam allowances in either direction.

🔍 Tip from a Super Sleuth

Do you have a gang of newbies who are borrowing sewing machines that they've never used? Do them and you a favor: start them out with pre-wound bobbins!

✱Clue 6 **1.** Gather three units completed in clue 4, the six units completed in clue 5, six large feature squares, and three feature rectangles. **2.** Sew three rows, beginning each row with a unit from clue 4 and ending with a feature rectangle as shown. Press the seam allowances toward the units from clue 4. This is row X.

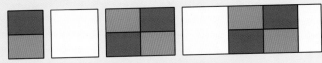

Clue 6. Row X: Assemble 3.

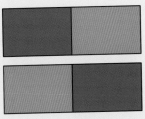

Clue 7. Make 4.

✱Clue 7 **1.** Gather eight units completed in clue 4. **2.** Sew four units as shown. Make sure the coordinate-A rectangles are positioned as shown. These are the mirror image of the units made in clue 5. Press the seam allowances in either direction.

Clue 8. Row Y: Assemble 2.

Clue 9. Row Z: Assemble 1.

✱Clue 8 **1.** Gather two units completed in clue 4, the four units completed in clue 7, four large feature squares, and two feature rectangles. **2.** Sew two rows, beginning each row with a feature rectangle and ending with a unit from clue 4 as shown. This is row Y.

✱Clue 9 **1.** Gather the remaining small feature square, two feature rectangles, two 4½" x 6½" coordinate-A rectangles, and three 4½" x 6½" coordinate-B rectangles. **2.** Sew one row, beginning with a small feature square and ending with a coordinate-B rectangle as shown. Make sure the coordinate-B rectangles are next to the feature fabrics. Press the seam allowances toward the feature square. This is row Z.

Wench support. Sherrie Tener, Mary MacCarter

Beefy Cabbage Comfort Casserole

This recipe is sheer comfort food! When you serve this, you'll need to make sure your sleuths don't just curl up with the blankies they are quilting and start to purr! This is perfect for the chilly winter gatherings!

1 head cabbage, chopped

1 lb. ground beef

1 onion, chopped

1 medium can corn, drained

1 small can sliced mushrooms, drained

1 medium can diced tomatoes (do not drain)

1 medium can tomato soup

1 cup uncooked rice (any kind)

Spread chopped cabbage across the bottom of a greased 9" x13" casserole dish. Sauté ground beef and onion until both are cooked through. Drain ground beef and onions. To this add sliced mushrooms, corn, diced tomatoes with its juice, tomato soup, and the uncooked rice. Stir all together and pour over the cabbage. Bake at 350° for 1 hour. Yum!! This will warm 6 hungry sleuths.

✳Clue 10 1. Lay out rows V–Z in the following order: row V, row W, row X, row W, row Y, row W, row X, row W, row Y, row W, row X, row W, row Z. Sew the rows together, and press the seam allowances in one direction. **2.** Examine the solutions on pages 62–91 to find the quilt photo and assembly diagram that match your completed quilt top. Add the borders and finish your quilt as described in your quilt's solution page.

TOP ABOVE: *My favorite part!* Ruth Ann Wiley, Shirley Schindler, Minnie Cousins, Judy Moyer, Diana Brewer

ABOVE: *Ta-Dah!* Katrina Robinson

LEFT: *Total concentration.* Brionne Gabis, Janine Gabis, Katrina Robinson, Karen Cydrus

Perplexing Watchword

The layout of this quilt reminds me of a puzzle in our daily newspaper. With this quilt you won't have to search for the correct letters and words, and you'll be a winner every time.

THE SUSPECTS

Your suspects will be cut from fabrics identified in the cutting list. For suggestions on fabric selection, see Identifying Your Fabrics on pages 7–8. This pattern does not lend itself well to directional fabrics.

All of the first cuts should be done with the fabric folded, selvage-to-selvage, as it comes off the bolt. Be sure to remove all selvage edges before making the first cuts.

Tracking your suspects

Arm yourself with a pen and a pad of sticky notes. Keep your suspects in groups as you cut them, and label the groups according to their fabric ID and piece sizes, as given in the List of Suspects.

SOLVING THE MYSTERY

Line up your groups of suspects. Set your machine for 10–15 stitches per inch (usually a setting of 2). Plug in your iron and don your sleuth cap!

Use the mug shots of your suspects to help you follow the clues to solving the mystery. Be sure to sew with a consistent ¼" seam allowance. You will find the solutions to the mystery quilts on pages 62–91.

feature   coordinate A   coordinate B   background

MUG SHOTS

Pieced top, 60" x 70"

LIST OF SUSPECTS			
Fabric ID	**Yardage**	**First Cut**	**Second Cut**
Feature	1⅞ yd.	6 strips 10½" x 40"	42 rectangles 5½" x 10½"
Coordinate A	⅔ yd.	7 strips 3" x 40"	84 squares 3" x 3"
Coordinate B	⅔ yd.	7 strips 3" x 40"	84 squares 3" x 3"
Background	1¼ yd.	7 strips 5½" x 40"	84 rectangles 3" x 5½"
Yardage based on 40" fabric width			
Additional fabric requirements for the borders, batting, backing, and binding are given in the solutions on pages 62–91.			

Clue 1. Make 84.

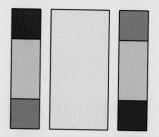

Clue 2. Block A: Make 21.

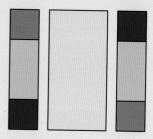

Clue 3. Block B: Make 21.

Slow-Cooker Potato-Corn Chowder

1 – 16 oz. bag frozen hash browns, thawed
1 chopped onion
8 slices bacon, fried crisp and crumbled
1 tsp. Worcestershire sauce
1 can shoe peg corn (undrained)
1 can cream-style corn
1 can roasted garlic flavored chicken broth
1½ cups milk (whole or skim)

Place all ingredients in slow cooker. Stir gently. Cook on low 6-8 hrs. Serve with sour cream or shredded cheese.

✱Clue 1 **1.** Gather 84 coordinate-A squares, 84 coordinate-B squares, and 84 background rectangles. **2.** Sew one coordinate-A and one coordinate-B square to the opposite ends of the background rectangle. Press the seam allowances toward the squares. Make 84.

✱Clue 2 **1.** Gather 42 units completed in clue 1 and 21 feature rectangles. **2.** Separate the units completed in clue 1 into two piles with 21 units in each pile. Lay the piles on opposite sides of the feature rectangles. Pay close attention to the positions of the background squares as shown. This is Block A. **3.** Sew two units completed in clue 1 to opposite long sides of the feature rectangles. Press the seams toward the feature rectangle.

✱Clue 3 **1.** Gather the remaining 42 units completed in clue 1 and the remaining 21 feature rectangles. **2.** Separate the units completed in clue 1 into two piles with 21 units in each pile. Lay the piles on opposite sides of the feature rectangles. Pay close attention to the positions of the background squares as shown. This is block B. Notice that block B is the mirror image of block A. **3.** Sew two units completed in clue 1 to opposite long sides of each feature rectangle. Press the seam allowances toward the feature rectangle.

Hint: *In these next two clues, notice that Block A is always vertical, Block B is always horizontal.*

❋Clue 4 **1.** Gather 12 blocks A and 12 blocks B. **2.** Sew four rows beginning with a vertical block A and ending with a horizontal block B as shown. Press the seam allowances in one direction. This is row X.

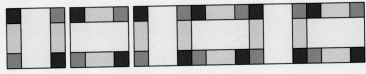

Clue 4. Row X: Assemble 4.

❋Clue 5 **1.** Gather the remaining nine blocks A and nine blocks B. **2.** Assemble three rows beginning with a horizontal block B and ending with a vertical block A as shown. Press the seam allowances in one direction. This is row Y.

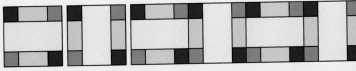

Clue 5. Row Y: Assemble 3.

Hint: *If you've sewn this pattern correctly, you'll note that all the cornerstones meet to form Four-Patches of alternating colors.*

❋Clue 6 **1.** Lay out the X and Y rows, alternating the rows, beginning and ending with an X row. Sew the rows together and press well. **2.** Examine the solutions on pages 62–91 to find the quilt photo and assembly diagram that match your completed quilt top. Add the borders and finish your quilt as described in your quilt's solution page.

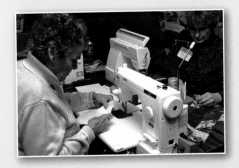

Tip from a Super Sleuth

Suggest that your sleuths make their mystery quilts from flannel....then put fleece on the back, with no batting in between. Cozy!!!

TOP ABOVE: *So careful!* Shirley Ayers, Sue Honeycutt
ABOVE: *The beautiful solution!* Vickie Rearley

Legend of the Missing Link

This quilt has more steps than most of the patterns in this book, but in the end it's worth it! As in life, when the last link in the chain joins again with the first, the task is complete. As you link the last chain in this mystery, you will have come full circle and made a beautiful quilt.

THE SUSPECTS

Your suspects will be cut from fabrics identified in the cutting list. For suggestions on fabric selection, see Identifying Your Fabrics on pages 7–8. Medium-to-large prints work well for the feature fabric. Directional prints are not recommended for this pattern.

All of the first cuts should be done with the fabric folded, selvage-to-selvage, as it comes off the bolt. Be sure to remove all selvage edges before making the first cuts.

Tracking your suspects

Arm yourself with a pen and a pad of sticky notes. Keep your suspects in groups as you cut them, and label the groups according to their fabric ID and piece sizes, as given in the List of Suspects.

SOLVING THE MYSTERY

Line up your groups of suspects. Set your machine for 10–15 stitches per inch (usually a setting of 2). Plug in your iron and don your sleuth cap!

Use the mug shots of your suspects to help you follow the clues to solving the mystery. Be sure to sew with a consistent ¼" seam allowance. You will find the solutions to the mystery quilts on pages 62–91.

feature   link fabric   chain fabric

MUG SHOTS

Pieced top, 51" x 63"

LIST OF SUSPECTS			
Fabric ID	**Yardage**	**First Cut**	**Second Cut**
Feature	2 yd.	3 strips 9½" x 40"	9 squares 9½" x 9½"
		3 strips 6½" x 40"	24 rectangles 3½" x 6½"
		1 strip 9½" x 40"	8 rectangles 3½" x 9½"
		2 strips 3½" x 40"	12 squares 3½" x 3½"
Link	⅔ yd.	2 strips 9½" x 40"	18 rectangles 3½" x 9½"
Chain	1⅝ yd.	5 strips 6½" x 40"	48 rectangles 3½" x 6½"
		3 strips 3½" x 40"	24 squares 3½" x 3½"
		1 strip 9½" x 40"	6 rectangles 3½" x 9½"
Yardage based on 40" fabric width			
Additional fabric requirements for the borders, batting, backing, and binding are given in the solutions on pages 62–91.			

✳Clue 1 **1.** Gather forty-eight 3½" x 6½" chain rectangles and twenty-four 3½" x 6½" feature rectangles. **2.** Sew two chain rectangles to opposite sides of each feature rectangle as shown. Press the seam allowances toward the rectangles.

Clue 1. Make 24.

✳Clue 2 **1.** Gather the 24 units completed in clue 1 and twelve 3½" x 9½" link rectangles. **2.** Sew two units completed in clue 1 to the opposite sides of each link rectangle . Press the seam allowances toward the link rectangles. This is block A.

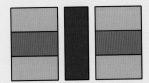

Clue 2. Block A: Make 12.

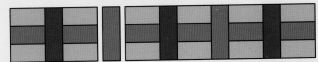

Clue 3. Row X: Make 4.

✳Clue 3 **1.** Gather eight 3½" x 9½" feature rectangles and 12 A blocks. **2.** Assemble four rows as shown. Each row will begin and end with an A block. Press the seam allowances toward the rectangles. This is row X.

Clue 4. Make 12.

✳Clue 4 **1.** Gather 24 chain squares and twelve 3½" x 3½" feature squares. **2.** Sew two chain squares to opposite sides of each feature square as shown. Press the seam allowances in one direction.

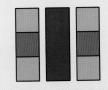

Clue 5. Block B: Make 6.

✳Clue 5 **1.** Gather six link rectangles and the 12 strips completed in clue 4. **2.** Sew two strips from clue 4 to the opposite long sides of each link rectangle. Press the seam allowances toward the link rectangles. This is block B.

Tip from a Super Sleuth

If you are hosting a Mystery Party and will be cutting kits, suggest that your sleuths move out of their comfort zone and try new combinations from the kits you cut!

Legend of the Missing Link

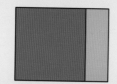

Clue 6. Block C: Make 6.

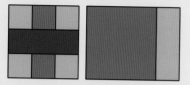

Clue 7. Unit X: Make 6.

Clue 8. Row Y: Make 3.

❋Clue 6 1. Gather the six chain rectangles and six 9½" x 9½" feature squares. **2.** Sew one chain rectangle to each feature square. Press the seam allowances toward the chain fabric. This is block C.

❋Clue 7 1. Gather six B blocks and six C blocks. **2.** Sew one B block to the feature-fabric side of each C block. Make sure to position the B block with the link rectangle set horizontally. **3.** Make six units, and press the seam allowances toward the feature square. This is unit X.

❋Clue 8 1. Gather six X units, and three 9½" x 9½" feature squares. **2.** Sew one unit X to opposite sides of each feature square . Make sure the row begins and ends with a chain rectangle. Press the seam allowances toward the center square. This is row Y.

❋Clue 9 1. Lay out the X and Y rows. Alternate the rows, beginning and ending with an X row. Sew the rows together. **2.** Examine the solutions on pages 62–91 to find the quilt photo and assembly diagram that match your completed quilt top. Add the borders and finish your quilt as described in your quilt's solution page.

Careful, careful... Sue Honeycutt

Treasure Amidst the Bric-a-Brac

Most of us have way more trinkets and whatnots than we know what to do with or have room to display. Quilts, on the other hand, are never clutter. This one reminds me of how quilts can tie the threads of our lives and friends together. We can never have too many quilts or too many friends.

THE SUSPECTS

Your suspects will be cut from fabrics identified in the cutting list. For suggestions on fabric selection, see Identifying Your Fabrics on pages 7–8. Directional prints are not recommended for the background and coordinates. Background fabric is quite a bit of the quilt and should be an interesting print.

All of the first cuts should be done with the fabric folded, selvage-to-selvage, as it comes off the bolt. Be sure to remove all selvage edges before cutting blocks.

Tracking your suspects

Arm yourself with a pen and a pad of sticky notes. Keep your suspects in groups as you cut them, and label the groups according to their fabric ID and piece sizes, as given in the List of Suspects.

SOLVING THE MYSTERY

Line up your groups of suspects. Set your machine for 10–15 stitches per inch (usually a setting of 2). Plug in your iron and don your sleuth cap!

Use the mug shots of your suspects to help you follow the clues to solving the mystery. Be sure to sew with a consistent ¼" seam allowance. You will find the solutions to the mystery quilts on pages 62–91.

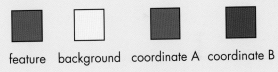

feature   background   coordinate A   coordinate B

MUG SHOTS

Pieced top, 48" x 56"

LIST OF SUSPECTS			
Fabric ID	**Yardage**	**First Cut**	**Second Cut**
Feature	¾ yd.	3 strips 8½" x 40"	12 squares 8½" x 8½"
Background	1½ yd.	3 strips 8½" x 40"	21 rectangles 4½" x 8½"
		2 strips 4½" x 40"	18 rectangles 2½" x 4½"
		5 strips 2½" x 40"	78 squares 2½" x 2½"
Coordinate A	½ yd.	2 strips 6½" x 40"	30 rectangles 2½" x 6½"
		1 strip 2½" x 40"	9 squares 2½" x 2½"
Coordinate B	½ yd.	2 strips 6½" x 40"	30 rectangles 2½" x 6½"
		1 strip 2½" x 40"	9 squares 2½" x 2½"
Yardage based on 40" fabric width			
Additional fabric requirements for the borders, batting, backing, and binding are given in the solutions on pages 62–91.			

Treasure Amidst the Bric-a-Brac

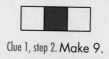

Clue 1, step 2. Make 9.

Clue 1, step 3. Make 9.

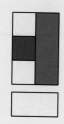

Clue 1, step 4. Unit 1: Make 9.

Clue 2, step 2. Make 9.

Clue 2, step 3. Make 9.

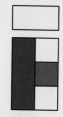

Clue 2, step 4. Unit 2: Make 9.

✳Clue 1 1. Gather eighteen 2½" x 2½" background squares, nine 2½" x 4½" background rectangles, nine coordinate-B squares, and nine coordinate-A rectangles. **2.** Sew two background squares to the opposite sides of each coordinate-B square as shown. Press the seam allowances in the same direction. Make nine strips. **3.** Sew a coordinate-A rectangle to each strip completed in step 2. Press the seam allowances toward the coordinate rectangle. **4.** Sew one 2½" x 4½" background rectangle to each unit completed in step 3 as shown. Pay close attention to the position of the coordinate pieces. Make sure the coordinate-A rectangle is on the right and the background rectangle is on the bottom. Press the seam allowances toward the background rectangle. This is unit 1, make nine.

✳Clue 2 1. Gather eighteen 2½" x 2½" background squares, nine 2½" x 4½" background rectangles, nine coordinate-A squares, and nine coordinate-B rectangles. **2.** Sew two background squares to the opposite sides of each coordinate-A square as shown. Press the seam allowances in one direction. Make nine strips. **3.** Sew a coordinate-B rectangle to each strip completed in step 2. Press the seam allowances toward the coordinate rectangle. **4.** Sew one 2½" x 4½" background rectangle to each unit completed in step 3 as shown. Pay close attention to the position of the coordinate pieces. Make sure the coordinate-B rectangle is on the left and the background rectangle is on the top. Press the seam allowances toward the background rectangle. This is unit 2, make nine.

✱Clue 3 1. Gather units 1 and 2 completed in clues 1 and 2. **2.** Assemble nine blocks as shown. Make sure to position unit 1 on the left with the background rectangle on the bottom and unit 2 on the right with the background rectangle on the top. Press the seam allowances in the same direction. This is block A.

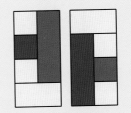

Clue 3. Block A: Assemble 9.

✱Clue 4 1. Gather the remaining forty-two 2½" x 2½" background squares, 21 coordinate-A rectangles, and 21 coordinate-B rectangles. **2.** Sew one background square to one end of each coordinate-A rectangle. Press the seam allowances in one direction. This is unit 3. **3.** Sew one background square to one end of each coordinate-B rectangle. Press the seam allowances in one direction. This is unit 4.

Clue 4, step 2. Unit 3: Make 21.

Clue 4, step 3. Unit 4: Make 21.

✱Clue 5 1. Gather 12 of the units 3 and 4 completed in clue 4, and twelve 4½" x 8½" background rectangles. **2.** Assemble 12 blocks as shown. Pay close attention to the position of each unit. Make sure unit 4 is on the top, with the coordinate-B rectangle on the left. And make sure unit 3 is on the bottom, with the coordinate-A rectangle on the right. Press the seam allowances toward the background rectangle. This is block B.

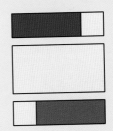

Clue 5. Block B: Assemble 12.

⊙ Tip from a Super Sleuth

If you have a Mystery Party for your guild or among your friends, try a carry-in or dessert-dinner (always a good thing in my book!!). Ask everyone to contribute food and share the recipe. Friends, food, and fun always make a good combination!

By golly...I did it! Amanda Howell, Janet Drake

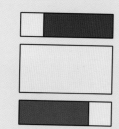

Clue 6. Block C: Assemble 9.

Clue 7. Row X: Assemble 4.

Clue 8. Row Y: Assemble 3.

White Chicken Chili

We seem to always have a good turnout of quilt detectives during the winter months. Perhaps it's because everyone has a bit of cabin fever. Maybe it's just that they are ready to hang out with friends and eat good food! This will certainly fit the bill!

3 – 14 oz. cans Great Northern beans, rinsed and drained

1 medium can creamed corn

1 small can chopped green chilies

1 medium can chicken broth

1 jar salsa, any size

1 cup shredded Monterey Jack cheese

1 store-cooked rotisserie chicken, skinned, boned, and shredded

Cook over medium heat on the stove top until heated through, or pour into slow cooker and cook all day on low. This serves 6 chilly sleuths.

✳Clue 6 **1.** Gather the remaining nine units 3 and 4 completed in clue 4, and nine 4½" x 8½" background bars. **2.** Assemble nine blocks as shown. Pay close attention to the position of each unit. Make sure unit 3 is on the top, with the coordinate-A rectangle on the right. Make sure unit 4 is on the bottom, with the coordinate-B rectangle on the left. Press the seam allowances toward the background rectangle. This is block C.

✳Clue 7 **1.** Gather the 12 B blocks completed in clue 5 and twelve 8½" x 8½" feature squares. **2.** Sew four rows with three B blocks and three feature squares. Alternate the squares with the blocks, beginning with a feature square and ending with a B block. Press the seam allowances toward the feature squares. This is row X.

✳Clue 8 **1.** Gather nine A blocks and nine C blocks. **2.** Sew three rows as shown. Alternate the blocks, beginning with a C block and ending with an A block. Pay close attention to the positions of the blocks. The coordinate-A rectangles in the C blocks should be on the upper left. The coordinate-B square in the A blocks should be on the left. Press the seam allowances in the same direction. This is row Y.

✳Clue 9 **1.** Lay out X and Y rows, alternating the rows, beginning and ending with an X row. Sew the rows together and press well. **2.** Examine the solutions on pages 62–91 to find the quilt photo and assembly diagram that match your completed quilt top. Add the borders and finish your quilt as described in your quilt's solution page.

Mystery on the Road Less Traveled

This super simple quilt leads you on a meandering path as you piece these strips and squares. The pattern that develops will remind you to take life at your leisure, and allow yourself to enjoy the journey.

THE SUSPECTS

Your suspects will be cut from fabrics identified in the cutting list. For suggestions on fabric selection, see Identifying Your Fabrics on pages 7–8. Directional prints are not recommended for this pattern.

All of the first cuts should be done with the fabric folded, selvage-to-selvage, as it comes off the bolt. Be sure to remove all selvage edges before making the first cuts.

Tracking your suspects

Arm yourself with a pen and a pad of sticky notes. Keep your suspects in groups as you cut them, and label the groups according to their fabric ID and piece sizes, as given in the List of Suspects.

SOLVING THE MYSTERY

Line up your groups of suspects. Set your machine for 10–15 stitches per inch (usually a setting of 2). Plug in your iron and don your sleuth cap!

Use the mug shots of your suspects to help you follow the clues to solving the mystery. Be sure to sew with a consistent ¼" seam allowance. You will find the solutions to the mystery quilts on pages 62–91.

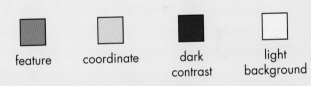

| feature | coordinate | dark contrast | light background |

MUG SHOTS

Pieced top, 48" x 60"

LIST OF SUSPECTS			
Fabric ID	**Yardage**	**First Cut**	**Second Cut**
Feature	1¼ yd.	3 strips 12½" x 40"	20 rectangles 4½" x 12½"
Coordinate	1¼ yd.	3 strips 12½" x 40"	20 rectangles 4½" x 12½"
Dark Contrast	½ yd.	3 strips 4½" x 40"	20 squares 4½" x 4½"
Light background	⅔ yd.	5 strips 4½" x 40"	40 squares 4½" x 4½"
Yardage based on 40" fabric width			
Additional fabric requirements for the borders, batting, backing, and binding are given in the solutions on pages 62–91.			

Mystery on the Road Less Traveled

Clue 1. Make 20.

✳Clue 1 **1.** Gather 20 dark contrast squares and 40 light background squares. **2.** Sew two background squares to the opposite sides of each contrast square as shown. Press the seam allowances in the same direction.

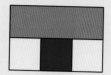

Clue 2. Make 20.

✳Clue 2 **1.** Gather 20 feature rectangles and the 20 strips completed in clue 1. **2.** Sew a feature rectangle to the top of each strip from clue 1 as shown. Press the seam allowances toward the feature rectangles.

Clue 3. Make 20.

✳Clue 3 **1.** Gather the units completed in clue 2 and the remaining 20 coordinating rectangles. **2.** Sew a coordinating rectangle to the bottom of each completed unit from clue 2 as shown. Press the seam allowances toward the coordinating rectangles. Make 20 blocks.

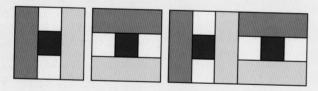

Clue 4. Row X: Make 3.

✳Clue 4 **1.** Gather 12 completed blocks from clue 3. **2.** Assemble a row of four blocks as shown. Pay close attention to the position of each block, beginning with a block positioned vertically. Rotate every other block ¼ turn to position it horizontally. Press the seam allowances to the right. This is row X. Make three.

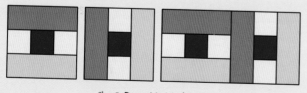

Clue 5. Row Y: Make 2.

✳Clue 5 **1.** Gather the remaining eight blocks from clue 3. **2.** Assemble a row of four blocks as shown. Pay close attention to the position of each block, beginning with a block positioned horizontally. Rotate every other block ¼ turn to position it vertically. Press the seam allowances to the left. This is row Y. Make two.

✳Clue 6 **1.** Lay out the rows X and Y. Alternate the rows, beginning and ending with a row X. Sew the rows together and press well. **2.** Examine the solutions on pages 62–91 to find the quilt photo and assembly diagram that match your completed quilt top. Add the borders and finish your quilt as described in your quilt's solution page.

BELOW LEFT: *I just love the colors.* Connie Leimbach, Connie Grounds, Janine Gabis, Brionne Gabis

BELOW CENTER: *Eat a little, sew a little.* Margaret Bradshaw, Pam Wysong, Connie Leimbach

BELOW RIGHT: *Last row!* Amanda Howell

Pasta Fruit Salad

This is a delicious light side dish for any gathering. It's particularly good in the springtime when we seem to start craving fruit. I love this because it's not too sweet.

8 oz. orzo pasta, cooked *al dente* and drained
1 large can crushed pineapple
1 small can mandarin oranges
1 medium can pears, chopped
1 cup seedless grapes, halved
⅓ cup sugar
2 tbsp. flour
2 eggs, beaten
1 8 oz. container whipped topping

As the pasta is cooking, drain all the fruits and reserve 1 cup total juice. After pasta is cooled, stir in the fruit. In small sauce pan combine juice, sugar, and flour and stir over medium heat. Gradually add the beaten eggs and continue to stir over the heat until thickened. Pour this sauce over the pasta and fruit and mix gently. Chill. Just before serving fold in whipped topping. This should feed 6 hungry detectives. With 6 sleuths in the room, we never seem to have leftovers.

Legend of the Spinning Top

WHIRLY-GIGS, 68" x 80".
Made by the staff at Creations SewClever, Chillicothe, Ohio

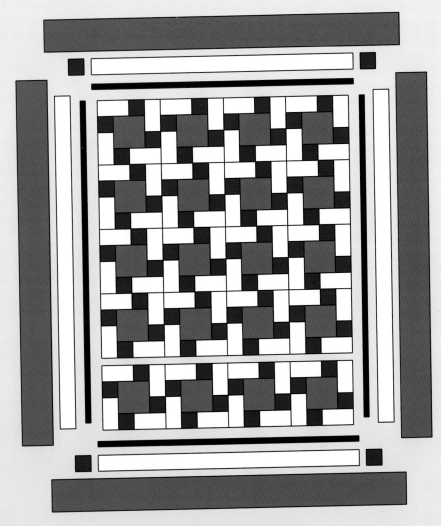

WHIRLY-GIGS, assembly diagram

✻ **Mystery solved.** Instructions for this quilt begin on page 17.
See the instructions on pages 92–93 for adding the borders to your quilt.

BORDER fabric IDs and finishing requirements		
Fabric ID	**Yardage**	**Cut**
Inner border: Black zinger (fabric not in pieced top)	⅜ yd.	6 strips 1½" x 40"
Middle border: Background	¾ yd.	6 strips 3½" x 40"
Outer border: Feature	1½ yd.	7 strips 6½" x 40"
Cornerstones: Contrast	scraps	4 squares 3½" x 3½"
Batting	one package twin-size batting	
Backing	4⅞ yd.	
Binding	⅔ yd.	

Mystery in the Antique Sewing Chest

RICK RACK, 64" x 76"
Made by the staff at Creations SewClever, Chillicothe, Ohio

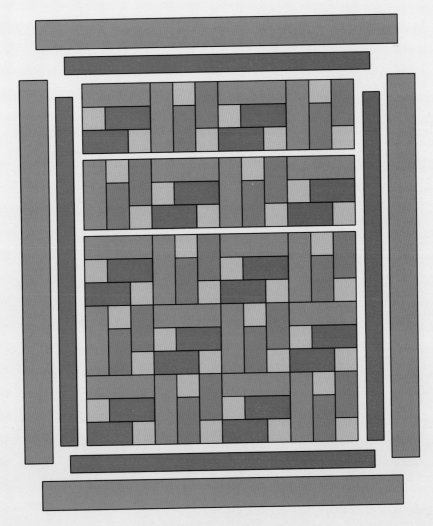

RICK RACK, assembly diagram

✳**Mystery solved.** Instructions for this quilt begin on page 20.
See the instructions on pages 92–93 for adding the borders to your quilt.

BORDER fabric IDs and finishing requirements		
Fabric ID	**Yardage**	**Cut**
Inner border: Coordinate A	⅝ yd.	6 strips 3½" x 40"
Outer border: Feature	1⅛ yd.	7 strips 5½" x 40"
Batting	one package twin-size batting	
Backing	4⅞ yd.	
Binding	⅔ yd.	

Clues Along the Uneven Path

COBBLESTONES, 64" x 76"
Made by the staff at Creations SewClever, Chillicothe, Ohio

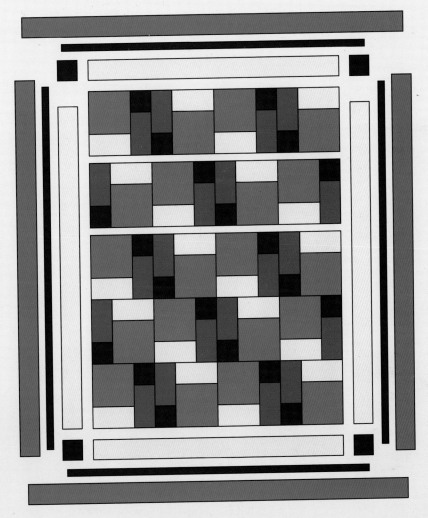

COBBLESTONES, assembly diagram

✳Mystery solved. Instructions for this quilt begin on page 23.
See the instructions on pages 92–93 for adding the borders to your quilt.

BORDER fabric IDs and finishing requirements		
Fabric ID	**Yardage**	**Cut**
Inner border: Background	⅝ yd.	6 strips 3½" x 40"
Middle border: Contrast	⅜ yd.	7 strips 1½" x 40"
Outer border: Feature	1 yd.	7 strips 4½" x 40"
Cornerstones: Contrast	scraps	4 squares 3½" x 3½"
Batting	one package twin-size batting	
Backing	4⅞ yd.	
Binding	⅔ yd.	

Secret in the Bureau Drawer

ARGYLE SOX, 61" x 79"
Made by the staff at Creations SewClever, Chillicothe, Ohio

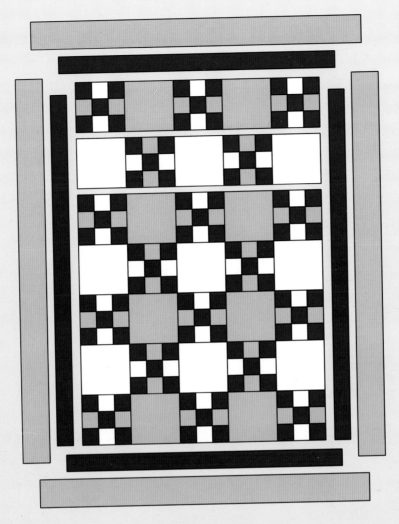

Argyle Sox, assembly diagram

*Mystery solved. Instructions for this quilt begin on page 25.
See the instructions on pages 92–93 for adding the borders to your quilt.

BORDER fabric IDs and finishing requirements		
Fabric ID	**Yardage**	**Cut**
Inner border: Contrast	¾ yd.	6 strips 3½" x 40"
Outer border: Feature	1¼ yd.	7 strips 5½" x 40"
Batting	one package twin-size batting	
Backing	4⅞ yd.	
Binding	⅔ yd.	

What Was in the Denim Jacket?

TWILL WEAVE, 64" x 82"
Made by the staff at Creations SewClever, Chillicothe, Ohio

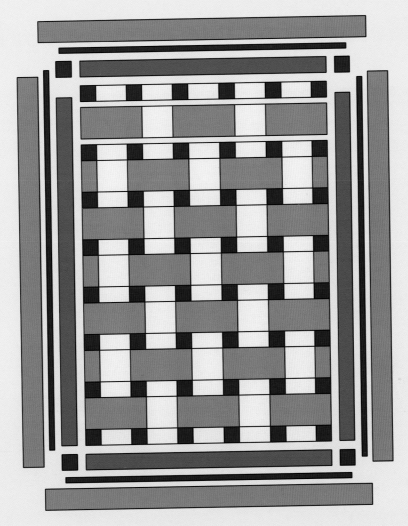

TWILL WEAVE, assembly diagram

✱Mystery solved. Instructions for this quilt begin on page 28.
See the instructions on pages 92–93 for adding the borders to your quilt.

BORDER fabric IDs and finishing requirements		
Fabric ID	**Yardage**	**Cut**
Inner border: Zinger (fabric not in pieced top)	¾ yd.	6 strips 3½" x 40"
Middle border: Contrast	⅜ yd.	7 strips 1½" x 40"
Outer border: Feature	1 yd.	7 strips 4½" x 40"
Cornerstones: Contrast	scraps	4 squares 3½" x 3½"
Batting	one package twin-size batting	
Backing	4⅞ yd.	
Binding	⅔ yd.	

Message in the Needlework

CROSS STITCH, 64" x 76"
Made by the staff at Creations SewClever, Chillicothe, Ohio

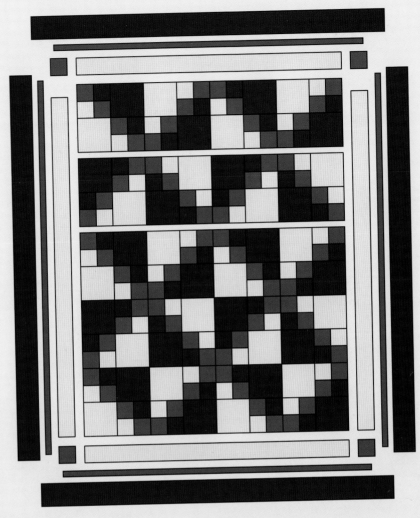

CROSS STITCH, assembly diagram

✳Mystery solved. Instructions for this quilt begin on page 30.

See the instructions on pages 92–93 for adding the borders to your quilt.

BORDER fabric IDs and finishing requirements		
Fabric ID	**Yardage**	**Cut**
Inner border: Coordinate	¾ yd.	6 strips 3½" x 40"
Middle border: Contrast	⅜ yd.	7 strips 1½" x 40"
Outer border: Feature	1 yd.	7 strips 4½" x 40"
Cornerstones: Contrast	scraps	4 squares 3½" x 3½"
Batting	one package twin-size batting	
Backing	4¾ yd.	
Binding	⅔ yd.	

The Deserted Highway

ROAD TO SPRINGFIELD, 64" x 76"
Made by the staff at Creations SewClever, Chillicothe, Ohio

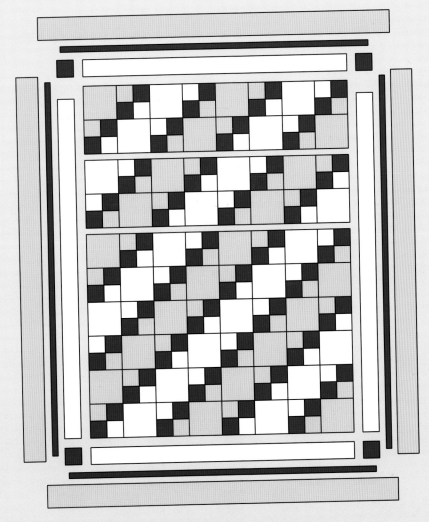

ROAD TO SPRINGFIELD, assembly diagram

❋Mystery solved. Instructions for this quilt begin on page 33.
See the instructions on pages 92–93 for adding the borders to your quilt.

BORDER fabric IDs and finishing requirements		
Fabric ID	**Yardage**	**Cut**
Inner border: Coordinate	¾ yd.	6 strips 3½" x 40"
Middle border: Contrast	⅜ yd.	7 strips 1½" x 40"
Outer border: Feature	1⅛ yd.	7 strips 4½" x 40"
Cornerstones: Contrast	scraps	4 squares 3½" x 3½"
Batting	one package twin-size batting	
Backing	4¾ yd.	
Binding	⅔ yd.	

The Baffling Basket Case

BASKET WEAVE, 70" x 79"
Made by the staff at Creations SewClever, Chillicothe, Ohio

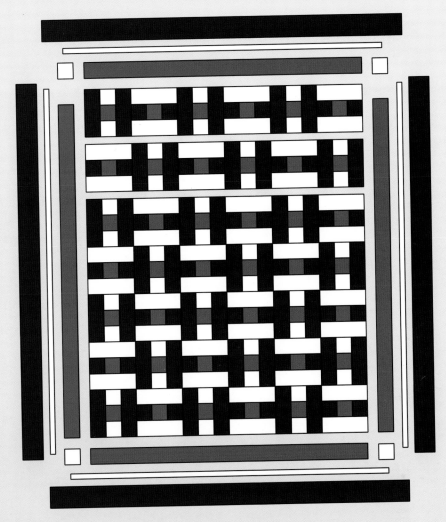

BASKET WEAVE, assembly diagram

❋Mystery solved. Instructions for this quilt begin on page 36.
See the instructions on pages 92–93 for adding the borders to your quilt.

BORDER fabric IDs and finishing requirements		
Fabric ID	**Yardage**	**Cut**
Inner border: Contrast	¾ yd.	6 strips 3½" x 40"
Middle border: Coordinate	⅜ yd.	7 strips 1½" x 40"
Outer border: Feature	1 yd.	8 strips 4½" x 40"
Cornerstones: Coordinate	scraps	4 squares 3½" x 3½"
Batting	one package twin-size batting	
Backing	4¾ yd.	
Binding	⅔ yd.	

Secret in the Sewing Box

WOVEN RIBBONS, 66" x 72"
Made by the staff at Creations SewClever, Chillicothe, Ohio

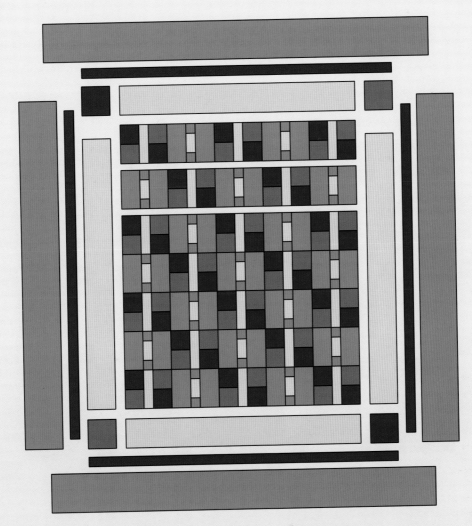

WOVEN RIBBONS, assembly diagram

＊Mystery solved. Instructions for this quilt begin on page 39.
See the instructions on pages 92–93 for adding the borders to your quilt.

BORDER fabric IDs and finishing requirements		
Fabric ID	**Yardage**	**Cut**
Inner border: Background	⅝ yd.	6 strips 3½" x 40"
Middle border: Coordinate A	⅜ yd.	7 strips 1½" x 40"
Outer border: Feature	1 yd.	7 strips 4½" x 40"
Cornerstones: Coordinates	scraps	4 squares 3½" x 3½"
Batting	one package twin-size batting	
Backing	4¾ yd.	
Binding	⅔ yd.	

Unexpected Playground Clue

HOPSCOTCH, 66" x 76"
Made by the staff at Creations SewClever, Chillicothe, Ohio

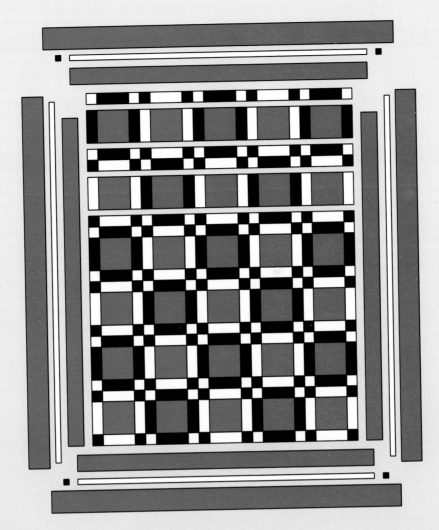

HOPSCOTCH, assembly diagram

✽Mystery solved. Instructions for this quilt begin on page 42.

See the instructions on pages 92–93 for adding the borders to your quilt.

BORDER fabric IDs and finishing requirements		
Fabric ID	**Yardage**	**Cut**
Inner border: Feature	⅝ yd.	6 strips 3½" x 40"
Middle border: Background	⅜ yd.	7 strips 1½" x 40"
Outer border: Feature	1 yd.	7 strips 4½" x 40"
Cornerstones: Dark contrast	scraps	4 squares 3½" x 3½"
Batting	one package twin-size batting	
Backing	4¾ yd.	
Binding	⅔ yd.	

What Became of Aunt Emma's Pinafore?

PIN DOTZ, 66" x 76"

Made by the staff at Creations SewClever, Chillicothe, Ohio

PIN DOTZ, assembly diagram

✽Mystery solved. Instructions for this quilt begin on page 45.

See the instructions on pages 92–93 for adding the borders to your quilt.

BORDER fabric IDs and finishing requirements		
Fabric ID	**Yardage**	**Cut**
Inner border: Coordinate B	⅞ yd.	6 strips 3½" x 40"
Outer border: Feature	1¼ yd.	7 strips 5½" x 40"
Cornerstones: Coordinate B	scraps	4 squares 3½" x 3½"
Batting	one package twin-size batting	
Backing	4¾ yd.	
Binding	⅔ yd.	

Perplexing Watchword

CROSSWORD PUZZLE, 76" x 86"
Made by the staff at Creations SewClever, Chillicothe, Ohio

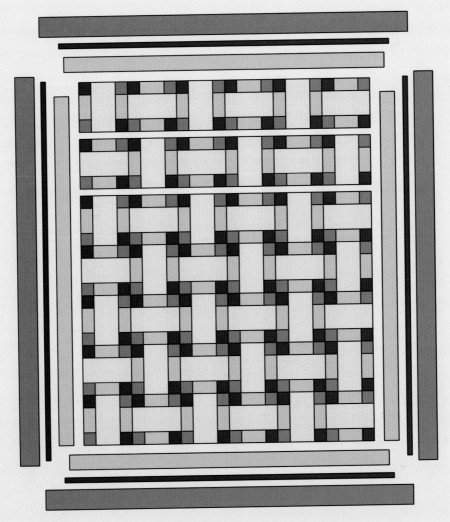

CROSSWORD PUZZLE, assembly diagram

✻Mystery solved. Instructions for this quilt begin on page 49.

See the instructions on pages 92–93 for adding the borders to your quilt.

BORDER fabric IDs and finishing requirements		
Fabric ID	**Yardage**	**Cut**
Inner border: Background	¾ yd.	7 strips 3½" x 40"
Middle border: Coordinate A	½ yd.	8 strips 1½" x 40"
Outer border: Coordinate B	1⅛ yd.	8 strips 4½" x 40"
Batting	one package twin-size batting	
Backing	4¾ yd.	
Binding	⅔ yd.	

Legend of the Missing Link

CHAIN LINK, 77" x 89"
Made by the staff at Creations SewClever, Chillicothe, Ohio

CHAIN LINK, assembly diagram

✻Mystery solved. Instructions for this quilt begin on page 52.

See the instructions on pages 92–93 for adding the borders to your quilt.

BORDER fabric IDs and finishing requirements		
Fabric ID	**Yardage**	**Cut**
Inner border: Feature	¾ yd.	7 strips 3½" x 40"
Second and fourth borders: Chain	1 yd.	14 strips 2" x 40"
Third border: Link	½ yd.	7 strips 1½" x 40"
Outer border: Feature	1⅛ yd.	7 strips 5½" x 40"
Batting	one package full-size batting	
Backing	5½ yd.	
Binding	¾ yd.	

Treasure Amidst the Bric-a-Brac

WHAT KNOTS? 64" x 72"
Made by the staff at Creations SewClever, Chillicothe, Ohio

WHAT KNOTS? assembly diagram

*Mystery solved. Instructions for this quilt begin on page 55.
See the instructions on pages 92–93 for adding the borders to your quilt.

BORDER fabric IDs and finishing requirements		
Fabric ID	Yardage	Cut
Inner border: Coordinate B	⅝ yd.	6 strips 3½" x 40"
Outer border: Feature	1¼ yd.	7 strips 5½" x 40"
Batting	one package twin-size batting	
Backing	4¾ yd.	
Binding	⅔ yd.	

Mystery on the Road Less Traveled

ZIGZAG, 64" x 76"
Made by the staff at Creations SewClever, Chillicothe, Ohio

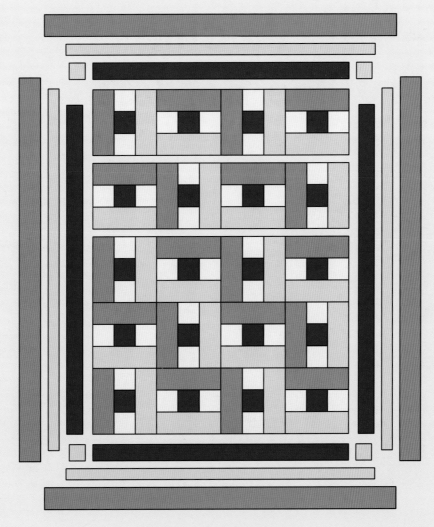

Zigzag, assembly diagram

*Mystery solved. Instructions for this quilt begin on page 59.

See the instructions on pages 92–93 for adding the borders to your quilt.

BORDER fabric IDs and finishing requirements		
Fabric ID	**Yardage**	**Cut**
Inner border: Dark contrast	⅝ yd.	6 strips 3½" x 40"
Middle border: Coordinate	⅜ yd.	7 strips 2½" x 40"
Outer border: Feature	1 yd.	7 strips 4½" x 40"
Cornerstones: Coordinate	scraps	4 squares 3½" x 3½"
Batting	one package twin-size batting	
Backing	4¾ yd.	
Binding	⅔ yd.	

Adding
the Borders

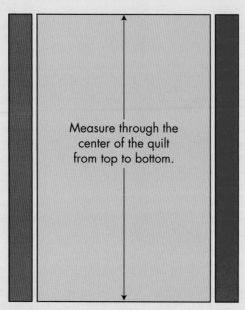

Fig. 1. Measure, cut, and sew on the side strips first.

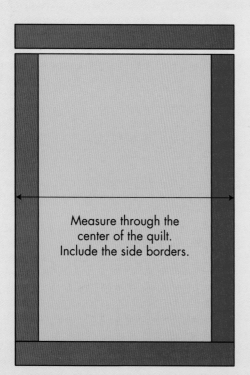

Fig. 2. Measure and cut the top and bottom strips.

Each of the quilts in this book has either two or three borders. The borders are applied one at a time, first the inner border, then the middle border, and finally, the outer border. Some of the borders are plain, and some have cornerstones.

Plain borders

1. Sew all of the strips for the border together, end-to-end, into one long piece. Press the seam allowances open.

2. Measure through the center of the quilt from top to bottom. Use this measurement to cut two strips for the sides of the border (Fig. 1).

3. Pin and sew these strips to the long sides of the quilt top, easing the edge of the quilt to fit the border strips. This will help square up the finished quilt and help it lie flat. Press the seam allowances toward the border strip.

4. Measure side-to-side across the center of the quilt top, including the newly added border.

5. Use this measurement to cut two more strips for the top and bottom of the border (Fig. 2).

6. Pin and sew these strips to the top and bottom of the quilt. Ease the edges of the quilt to fit the border strips. Press the seam allowances toward the borders.

Cornerstone borders

Cornerstones are added to the top and bottom strips. This changes the way you measure the top and bottom strips.

1. Sew all of the strips for the first border together, end-to-end, into one long piece. Press the seam allowances open.

2. Measure through the center of the quilt from top to bottom. Use this measurement to cut two strips for the sides of the border, but do not sew them to the quilt yet. Measure from side-to-side through the center of the quilt. Use this measurement to cut the top and bottom strips (Fig. 3).

3. Gather the four cornerstone squares that you cut according to the instructions in your pattern. Sew a cornerstone to the ends of the top and bottom strips. Press the seam allowances toward the cornerstones.

4. Sew the side strips to the quilt top and press the seam allowances toward the border strips. Then sew the top and bottom strips completed in step 3 and press the seam allowances toward the border strips (Fig. 4).

FINISHING YOUR QUILT

More and more quilters today enjoy turning the finishing chores over to someone with a long-arm quilting machine. This means they have the pleasure of selecting the fabrics and making the quilt top. Then they deliver the backing and binding fabric, along with the batting, to the longarm quilter, who will install the quilt on the machine and finish the quilting. Some services include finishing the binding. But it's easy enough to apply binding, and you may want to do it yourself.

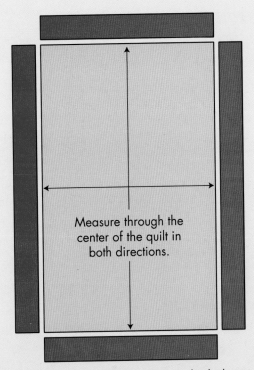

Fig. 3. Measure through the center in both directions.

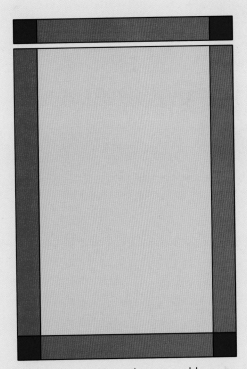

Fig. 4. Sew cornerstones to the top and bottom border strips.

MORE MYSTERY CLASS ANECDOTES
Dry White Wine

Our shop employee Vicki is a wonderful gal who is delightfully naive. She's also our "super-cook" for the Mystery Classes. One day during a shop lunch hour, Vicki said to me, as about six of us sat around our big cutting table eating our lunches, "Rita, I wanted to make that chicken recipe you had on the e-mail this week, but I wasn't able to find all the ingredients."

I replied, "Well, everything was from the local grocery store. What was it that you couldn't find?"

"Dry white wine," she replied with consternation.

"Vicki, dry white wine is in every grocery store," many of us said in unison.

"Hmmmm," she pondered. "I looked in the powdered drink aisles of three different grocery stores and simply couldn't find it!"

Well, She's Really Crafty

My oldest daughter called one afternoon and said she had about eight friends from work who asked if I'd put a Mystery Class together for them. I was thrilled to think of a classroom full of twenty-somethings, and I said, "Absolutely. But since it's such a huge amount of work to put on a Mystery Class, how about if I open it to other interested folks?" She was in complete agreement and added that she wanted her other two sisters and her brother's girlfriend to come, too. "That will be tons of fun," I replied. I called our son and said, "Erin asked if Laine could come to a Mystery Class next Sunday. Do you know if she can sew?"

He replied, "Hmmm, I don't know if she can sew. I think so. She's really crafty."

I got color requests from all the sleuths and had kits cut and ready for our impromptu Mystery Class. Laine, whom I really didn't know well yet, came in with my daughters. "Have you ever sewn before, Laine?" I asked. "Um, well a little bit a long time ago," she answered shyly. I set a machine up for her and got it all threaded. I told her to go ahead and sit at the machine, and I'd be right over to show her the basics. My first inkling that this was all new to her came as I saw her pull her chair up to the wrong side of the sewing machine. I smiled inwardly and gently turned the machine around to face her. Then I grabbed our most patient wench and assigned her to Laine full-time. Although Laine was not a skilled seamstress, David was right, she was crafty. She caught on quickly and she not only completed her mystery quilt, but enlarged it and made a queen-size quilt top. She was weary but very pleased as we wound down the day.

Several weeks later we attended Laine's college graduation party. My gift was to quilt and bind her Mystery top, and I wrapped it gaily and presented it to her the night before her party. She was completely amazed at what she had accomplished. The next evening at her party, the backdrop for the cake table was her beautiful quilt hanging on the wall. The first words out of everyone's mouth were not, "Congratulations on your college graduation," but rather, "I can't believe you made this quilt!"

P. S. Laine is now my delightful daughter-in-law!

This is my absolute favorite. Sharon Shuler

Meet the Author

Rita is a nationally known speaker and teacher, and president of Creations SewClever, Inc., in Chillicothe, Ohio. She's a native of Northeastern Ohio with a B.A. in clothing & textiles/business from the University of Akron. Rita, her husband, Ron, and their four children lived for many years in the Desert Southwest where she was a clothing designer and custom seamstress. In the late 1980s, the family relocated to a small farm in rural southern Ohio. It was the perfect place to raise a family, but there was not much demand for a custom dressmaker. In 1992 a wonderful opportunity presented itself and Rita bought a small quilt shop. She had discovered the career of her dreams! All of the quilts shown in this book evolved from the many Mystery Classes Rita has taught over the years. When designing the pattern for a Mystery Class, the quilt needs to be completed in one afternoon and be easy for quilters of any skill level. The quilt patterns contained in this book are from the Sunday Mystery Classes at Creations SewClever. We hope you'll reach a solution that delights you!

Today Creations SewClever is a busy quilt shop with a fabulous, friendly, funny staff of over 20 people. If you ever find yourself in southern Ohio, be sure to stop by the old funeral home now known as Creations SewClever. Rita and her friendly staff are dying to show you around!

Rita's Fast Fake Cheesecake

Every gathering of quilting sleuths involves a dessert. Of course at least one of them is chocolate. This recipe is always my contribution, usually made up at the very last minute.

1 ready-made angel food cake
1 8 oz. pkg. cream cheese, softened
1 8 oz. container whipped topping, thawed
1 large can fruit pie filling

Tear the angel food cake into bite sized pieces and put into very large mixing bowl. In a separate bowl, using an electric mixer, beat the softened cream cheese, gradually adding the whipped topping. Mix thoroughly. Pour over the torn angel food cake pieces and fold gently until mixed well. Spread evenly into 9" x 13" casserole and top with fruit. Chill before serving. This tastes remarkably like a light, fruity cheesecake and guests will want to lick the bottom of the pan! Serves 6 to 8.

Other AQS Books

This is only a small selection of the books available from the American Quilter's Society. AQS books are known worldwide for timely topics, clear writing, beautiful color photos, and accurate illustrations and patterns. The following books are available from your local bookseller, quilt shop, or public library.

#7078   us$24.95

#7075   us$21.95

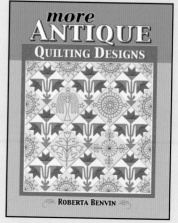

#6907   us$21.95

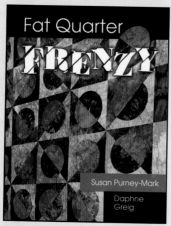

#6673   us$21.95

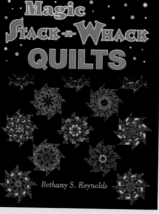

#4995   us$19.95

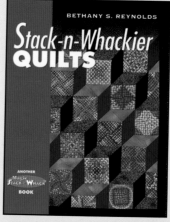

#5850   us$21.95

#7014   us$24.95

#6800   us$22.95

#6799   us$22.95